Praise for *Bible in Ten*

CW01024452

'I wish the brilliant *Bible in Ten* had been written sooner – it to read but with so much packed in. Whatever your biblical value for you. Dave Kitchen has put in the hard miles of study ing the big picture. Thanks, Dave!'
Abby Guinness, head of Spring Harvest

'What a wonderful idea Dave Kitchen has come up with. I have known Dave for over 35 years and he has not lost any of his enthusiasm and quirky sharing of the good news of God's love. This will be a valuable resource in my present multicultural context, giving people an instant insight into the scriptures and hopefully a desire to go deeper through Bible study and teaching. I warmly commend this book.'
Stephen Poxon, past president of the Methodist Conference and minister of St Mark's Methodist Church in Tottenham

'Such an exciting initiative. I love *Bible in Ten*.'
Rob Parsons, OBE

'Here's a version of the Bible which sets out to catch your attention – but goes on to engage your imagination and offer a fresh perspective on some familiar passages: thoroughly recommended.'
Stephen Wigley, chair of Wales Synod Cymru of the Methodist Church

'Very helpful, easy-to-read resource that I would encourage both young and old to invest in. It will certainly be a book that I will be keeping within reaching distance on my bookshelf.'
Ishmael, singer-songwriter, speaker and author

'Tackling the Bible can feel like a mammoth task and I certainly have often wondered where to start. Well, look no further! I love that this book has a mini summary at the end of each section, adding context and a little life reflection about what each book of the Bible has shared with us. Also, purely on a selfish note… this is on point for a dyslexic. Small, accessible, bite-sized pieces of an extremely large, comprehensive and complex book, and this helps to make some sense of it in the here and now. I want to share this with everyone I know.'
Megan Thomas, Methodist Youth President 2014–15

'Brilliant! So pithy and relevant. What a fantastic achievement – love those final paragraphs at the end of the chapter, communicating the very essence of the book. Sure it's going to be a real success!'
Rae Duke, broadcaster, teacher and podcast host

15 The Chambers, Vineyard
Abingdon OX14 3FE
brf.org.uk

Bible Reading Fellowship is a charity (233280)
and company limited by guarantee (301324),
registered in England and Wales

ISBN 978 1 80039 151 2
First published 2023
10 9 8 7 6 5 4 3 2 1 0

Text © David Kitchen 2023
This edition © Bible Reading Fellowship 2023
Cover illustrated by Ben Bloxham

The author asserts the moral right to be identified as the author of this work

Acknowledgements
Every effort has been made to trace and contact copyright owners for material used in this resource.
We apologise for any inadvertent omissions or errors, and would ask those concerned to contact us
so that full acknowledgement can be made in the future.

A catalogue record for this book is available from the British Library

Printed and bound in the UK by Zenith Media NP4 0DQ

DAVID KITCHEN

BIBLE IN TEN

ANY BOOK OF THE BIBLE
CRACKED IN TEN MINUTES OR LESS

BRF

Also available as an audiobook, narrated by David Kitchen, George Craig, Cathy Gale, Trystan Owain Hughes, Jennie Hurd, Roy Jenkins, Rob Parsons, Iwan Russell-Jones, Karen Walker, Olivia Warburton, Jenny Wigley and Stephen Wigley.

Head to Audible for your copy.

Do you have ten minutes?
Get your head around any book of the Bible.
It's a start, of course, not a finish.
This is big picture stuff – the highlights in the headlights,
plus a rummage around the corners.
What you'll see has always been there,
but it's surprising what people can miss.
Ten minutes and a door can open.
Go on, try it…

Contents

Introduction 9

The big picture: a quick look at the whole book 11

OLD TESTAMENT

Genesis: start the clock 16

Exodus: trouble and travel 22

Leviticus: the priest book 28

Numbers: doing detail, getting sorted 32

Deuteronomy: choose life 36

Joshua: renewing the promise 41

Judges: could do better 45

Ruth: love's journey 50

1 Samuel: kingmaker and kings 55

2 Samuel: rise and fall 61

1 Kings: notes from exile 66

2 Kings: down and down 72

1 Chronicles: a place to call your own 77

2 Chronicles: more than buildings 81

Ezra: come this far, still so far to go 85

Nehemiah: putting it right 88

Esther: special delivery 93

Job: nightmare days 98

Psalms: soul music 103

Proverbs: electricity for the brain 109

Ecclesiastes: life before death... 115

Song of Songs: the word is love 118

Isaiah: the light and the dark 121

Jeremiah: chaos creeps closer... 127

Lamentations: long time down... 132

Ezekiel: hard times but grand designs 137

Daniel: dream central 141

Hosea: love never gives up.. 148

Joel: back from the edge... 152

Amos: not expected, not wanted... 154

Obadiah: family fallout... 157

Jonah: a whale of a time 158

Micah: all that lies ahead.. 161

Nahum: it's over.. 164

Habakkuk: wheels turning 166

Zephaniah: not just all the others.. 168

Haggai: halfway is nowhere 170

Zechariah: endings and beginnings 172

Malachi: turn to God 176

NEW TESTAMENT

A word about the gospels.. 180

Matthew: good news in the family.. 181

Mark: lots to do, must dash... 188

Luke: outsiders on the inside 196

John: the word is out..205

The Acts of the Apostles: what, where, how?.....................214

Romans: thinking it through 222

1 Corinthians: a better way 226

2 Corinthians: make room in your hearts.........................230

Galatians: old rules and new lives 234

Ephesians: the heart of the message................................237

Philippians: a thank you in troubled times 240

Colossians: complicated isn't clever 243

1 Thessalonians: in the right direction 246

2 Thessalonians: stay in the today 248

1 Timothy: sense, not nonsense 250

2 Timothy: your turn now..253

Titus: necessary, practical, useful....................................256

Philemon: slave or brother?..258

Hebrews: keep the faith 260

James: you say it's real, show me......................................264

1 Peter: stick with it 267

2 Peter: get a grip 270

1 John: the real Jesus..272

2 John: keep love going...275

3 John: the difference you make..276

Jude: taking advantage...277

Revelation: where all our journeys end.............................279

Further reading 282

Acknowledgements...286

Introduction

When Bibles first came off the early printing presses, they were so precious they had to be chained down to keep them safe. In fact, some of them were so heavy you'd be doing very well to lift them, never mind move them. These days, there are millions in circulation but they seem to be read less and less. So, if you think David and Goliath is the name of a ship, you wouldn't be alone. Then how about Mahlah, Hoglah and Tirzah? Important women whose role in history is often forgotten.

Bible in Ten gives you a short, sharp snapshot of every single book in the Bible. Each one of them should take around ten minutes to read, often less. They concentrate on explaining what happens – springboards for getting to know the whole story better. It's a way to step aside from the chapters and verses by which the Bible was divided up centuries ago and to briefly see each book as a whole.

The word 'Bible' simply means 'books' and there are all sorts within this library. They range from short, personal notes to massive histories, from poetry to politics. It's a library which covers not only different places but very different times as well.

Overviews like this don't answer every question you will ever have about the Bible. Thousands of years of debate can't be neatly resolved in a few minutes. But what you should have by the end of the book is a much clearer idea of what the Bible contains. Hopefully, you'll also sense how beautiful, astonishing and unpredictable God's library is.

Reading this book obviously isn't the same as reading the whole Bible, but it's a start for understanding it. When thousands of years stand between you and the writers, some things will inevitably sound strange. Historically, you're being taken back in some cases to times when people thought human sacrifice was a necessary requirement for the health and well-being of a community.

Almost as alien to modern eyes was the situation regarding slavery. It seems so abhorrent today but, back then, slave labour was not necessarily forced labour. Slaves were not actually at the bottom of the jobs pyramid. That place belonged to the hired hands who got casual work on a daily basis with no rights to fall back on. If the work dried up, they went hungry: a gig economy for ancient times. In contrast, slaves with responsible masters and mistresses had guaranteed food, shelter and safety. There were laws that protected them. Of course, bad masters and mistresses were a very different matter and the full horrors of that were every bit as bad as today.

That's one small example of how it's not always easy to understand a situation that occurred thousands of years ago. To help you look deeper into the detail and the issues that the Bible raises, there's a section headed 'Further reading' at the end of this book. Some of the suggestions are much bigger reads than others, but all of them have their enthusiastic supporters, so take a look and decide what might be right for you.

Let us know how you use this book, what you like, plus what else you've found yourself by emailing **bibleinten@brf.org.uk**. We don't guarantee to reply individually to every single email, but we do promise to take a look and pass on the best suggestions for using this material and getting to know the Bible better.

Finally, a word from the writer of Ecclesiastes, who warned that constant study can actually wear you out. So give the Bible your time, but remember that it's there for you to enjoy, not in order to make you exhausted.

The big picture:
a quick look at the whole book

This is a library of surprises with God at the heart, an absolute bundle of useful stuff: guidance, comment, rules… but over two-thirds of it is poetry and story. It begins with shape out of chaos, light out of dark, a paradise to call home.

Then someone wants more than they should have and the trouble starts. Heroes seem hard to find. Noah's a good man in dark times; Abraham goes where God sends him – but much of the early story is about families who squabble and compete.

Freedom becomes slavery and life looks bleak, but Moses leads the escape on a long road to the promised land. The rules never seem to be kept, the battles are gruesome, but not everyone behaves badly. Ruth marries Boaz in a love story that leads directly to King David and finally to Jesus of Nazareth.

Straighten it up

As time passes, people decide they want a king like other nations. Bad idea! King Saul is not to be trusted; David's fine in battle but not great at home; Solomon starts wisely but ends stupidly. A few are good; many are dreadful; some don't make any obvious sense at all. Zimri sets fire to his own palace and himself in only seven days and Queen Athaliah tries to kill all her own grandchildren.

The people are told again and again to get rid of what stands between them and God. 'Hate what is evil. Love what is right,' demands Amos. 'Stop doing religion and start doing fairness.'

It's not all doom and gloom. 'If there's any hope, any protection, any safe place in times of trouble,' says Isaiah, 'it comes from God. There will be a day when flowers bloom in the wild places and those who are worn out will be tired no more. A way back to God will open up for all who love him.'

Calling out

There's joy among the poems, too. Psalm 30 says:

> I was as low as it gets… you lifted me.
> I needed help so badly… you healed me.
> I was staring over the edge… you held on to me.
> That's why I sing, that's why I feel secure:
> Because I called and you answered,
> Because you took my tears and made me dance again.

On top of that, you've got the best part of a thousand wise one-liners like: 'Talk without thought can cut and hurt, but wise words heal the heart.'

Job shouts that he wishes God had just let him die and the writer of Ecclesiastes struggles to see what life is all about. But, even when there are no answers, there is hope. Zechariah sees a peacemaker coming who will put things right.

When the people are taken as slaves to Babylon, that must have seemed like a ridiculous dream. Even when they returned home, it wasn't easy. The prophets' message was simple at heart: get sorted, stay right, be God's people. But something always got in the way and eventually there seems to be no more to say. Four hundred years pass when there isn't a single word recorded from God's messengers.

Backstreet beginnings

Part II begins in a Bethlehem backstreet with the cry of a tiny child. Jesus is poor, becomes an exile and is without connections, but when he grows up and tells it like it is, people are astonished. There's power in him: the lame walk, the blind see, the hungry are fed. No wonder crowds turn up in their thousands.

Sadly, they don't always like the message itself. Jesus offers forgiveness and a new start. He tells them he's the bread of life. That's too much of a claim. Even some of his own family want to put him away quietly.

The Jesus stories are sharp-edged tales. Bad boys come good and the so-called good ones don't match them. Much of it is about who needs help. If a shepherd has lost one of his sheep, doesn't he go out looking for it? If someone who is lost can be found, God's heart overflows with joy.

It's not over

Support for Jesus grows and, when he returns to Jerusalem one spring for the Passover festival, he has hundreds of supporters. The bad news is that he also has enemies in high places. Being different is dangerous and he pays for his criticism of the establishment with his life. The leaders fix up his crucifixion, the nails are hammered in and the story is over.

Or is it?

Thirty-six hours after his burial, Mary Magdalene comes back from a visit to his tomb, declaring breathlessly to his friends that the 'dead' body isn't there and she's actually met Jesus again. Bit by bit, a remarkable truth becomes clear. Death isn't the end. He's back and a new chapter is starting where his followers become his messengers.

Worldwide wonder

At the heart of this change is Paul, a most unusual man. He starts out as a key enemy of Christ's followers but meets Jesus on the Damascus Road. In time, he becomes the one who takes the news worldwide – the great traveller, speaker and letter-writer who is able to capture the heart of what it's all about.

'The wonder of this life is that Christ lives in you,' he explains. 'When we were helpless, he became our help. Astonishing! Even though we don't deserve anything, his life and death mean we can be forgiven and start again. So, if we walk this road, we do it together in faithfulness and with Jesus.'

Paul knows that the followers of Jesus he meets are not simply part of a workforce but part of a family. Other writers do their bit as well. James is great on what we say and do; John knows love is what you need and Peter deals with living on earth while never forgetting heaven.

The library ends with a vision of better times to come. One day, all the bad will burn away like paper in a fire and only the good will remain. No more crying, no more grief, no more death: a new world without dark corners, a life beyond shadows.

The journey seems long and complicated, but the heart of the story isn't. In the beginning, God creates us; at the end, if we turn to him, he welcomes us home.

OLD TESTAMENT

Genesis:
start the clock

Back at the start, the different parts of the Bible didn't have titles. As time went by, the writings became known by particular names and were then divided into chapters and verses. The title 'Genesis' means beginning. A pretty straightforward choice that's hard to argue with.

In the beginning, nothing at all… except the breath of God making a world of sea and sky, night and day with creatures of all shapes and sizes. Then there's a man and a woman in the garden of Eden and just one fruit not to eat. But it only needs one. The snake in the grass is the voice that whispers: 'Go on, try it out.' Adam blames Eve, Eve blames the snake. Nobody blames themselves.

So it's exit paradise, enter the world we know. Adam and Eve have two sons called Cain and Abel, brothers who – naturally – compete with each other. When Cain doesn't fully follow God's way of doing things but Abel does, it would have been easy for Cain to put it right. Instead, jealousy leads to another line being crossed. Cain murders his own brother.

Later, Adam and Eve have another son called Seth. There are family histories in which you learn that Seth had a son called Enosh, who had a son called Kenan, who had a… well, you know how lists work. After that, it's back to problems with people and it might be fair to ask if God himself could be wondering why on earth he'd started all this in the first place.

The answer is Noah. One good person makes all the difference. Build a boat before the storm comes, God tells him, and round up some animals. Everyone laughs until the rains arrive. This is the flood of all your worst nightmares. When it's over, God says, 'Never again,' and tells Noah that a rainbow will be a reminder of his promise.

For a while, the world is clean again. But good news never lasts long here. Instead of wanting to make a space for God, people end up wanting to make a name for themselves by building towers into the heavens. So God lets language become a source of confusion instead of communication.

The man with two names

Generations go by before God spots a man called Abram. He asks him to swap the family home for a land where he'll be happy and make others happy too. Abram says 'yes', gets there and what happens? Famine! So they move on to live in Egypt for a time.

Finally, back in Canaan, Abram grows wealthy, but the family grows too. Cousins are crammed together – like Christmas but all year round. So Abram and his nephew Lot agree to go in different directions. Lot is given first choice and takes the area with the fancy cities. Abram has what's left but God promises that this is the land where his family will just keep on growing, which sounds unlikely because Abram is old and has no sons.

God tells him not to worry, but he does and, at his wife Sarah's suggestion, he gets her maidservant Hagar pregnant. Hagar has a son, Ishmael, but jealousy rears its ugly head and Sarah blames Abram for doing what she suggested. In all this, God sticks by Abram and even gives him a new name – Abraham – meaning 'father of many nations'.

Meanwhile, Lot's family are living in stylish Sodom which has a great nightlife… if you don't have any morals. So God condemns the city and tells them to leave without looking back. Lot escapes from the destruction but his wife looks back and is turned into a pillar of salt. These are tough times where Abraham discovers that you can talk to God in prayer even when you feel you don't understand or even agree with him.

Eventually the big moment: Sarah gives Abraham a son, Isaac. God looks after him but he also cares about the son Abraham had with Sarah's servant. Years pass, there are disputes and peace treaties, good and bad times. Then one day God says: 'Abraham, I want you to sacrifice your son Isaac to me.'

Abraham says nothing. Well, what could he say? Suddenly God's promises sound very hollow, but Abraham follows the command to go to a mountain in Moriah. This was an age when human sacrifice was not unusual. People thought the gods required it. Abraham prepares himself but, at the last moment, God steps in with a sheep instead of a son. God now knows that Abraham is committed to him, every step of the way. Abraham knows that human life is precious and that God will provide.

Two brothers

After that, it's back to family history with a long list of great names like Milcah, Pildash, Uz and Buz. Sarah dies, Isaac marries, Abraham dies, Isaac has children: another pair of brothers and, yes, more competition.

Esau is the outdoor type, a big hunter and his father's favourite; Jacob is quieter, looks after the sheep and his mother likes him best. However, he's devious. One day, Jacob gets Esau to swap his rights as the firstborn for a bowl of bean stew – probably the most expensive meal in world history. Then he fools his elderly dad into blessing him rather than his brother.

Esau says: 'Right – when our father's dead and buried, you're next.' Jacob has only one choice: get out fast. On the run, he has a dream. God promises him that, in spite of his crooked ways, he can still have a place in his plans. Wherever Jacob may be, God will be there too.

So he grows up far away from home and learns first-hand what it's like to be cheated himself. Eventually the time comes when he has to face up to what he did and he decides to try to make peace with his brother. To his amazement, it's possible. Esau wants to be friends. The past, you see, has to be left in the past: not so much forgotten as forgiven.

Of course, it's not all plain sailing and pretty sunsets. But somehow Jacob's faith survives and he gets an extra name: Jacob, the deceiver, becomes Israel, the one who will not let go of God.

Dream weaving

After the trouble between him and Esau, you would have thought that Jacob would know the danger of having favourites. But some families never learn. One of Jacob's twelve sons gets special treatment: Joseph. The other brothers hate him because he tells Jacob what they're up to, has a fabulous multicoloured coat and dreams he's going to be far greater than they are.

The brothers want him out of the way. Once they've trapped him, their first plan is to dump him at the bottom of an old dried-up well to starve, but eventually they sell him to slave traders.

Surprisingly, it doesn't work out so badly for Joseph. He ends up in Egypt, working for a senior government official called Potiphar who likes this bright and reliable newcomer. Life is fine until Potiphar's wife takes a fancy to the young servant. He says 'no' but lands up in jail for what he didn't do! Not fair, of course, but life rarely is in the short-term.

In prison, he helps people understand what their dreams mean. Impressive… but it doesn't save him. At least, not until Pharaoh, the king, has a dream and no one can help him. Suddenly one of his staff remembers the dream-solver from the prison. 'I know who can help,' he says. 'His name's Joseph and he'll tell you exactly what it's about.'

In next to no time, Joseph is scrubbed up and bundled into Pharaoh's presence to hear weird stories about cattle and corn swallowing each other up. 'I can't tell you what they mean,' he says, 'but God can. It's about the good years and the famine that will follow.'

The king's impressed: Joseph goes from local prisoner to governor of Egypt in 24 hours. His job description: food management and distribution. The good years come but don't last forever, the famine strikes and guess who turns up? Joseph's brothers. His family are starving back in Canaan so Jacob has sent his sons to hunt for food, all of them apart from the youngest, Benjamin, his new favourite.

A twist in the tale

Joseph recognises his brothers, although they don't recognise him. In fact, they've assumed he's dead. He gives them the food they need but demands that one brother, Simeon, remains under arrest until they bring Benjamin to show that the story they have told him is true. When they get back home, the brothers realise that someone has put the money they paid for the food back in their bags. Jacob is furious: 'First I lose Joseph, then Simeon. Now you want to take Benjamin back there? Are you trying to make me lose all my sons?'

So Simeon remains in Egypt while Jacob's family slowly get hungrier. Although Jacob doesn't want to let Benjamin go, he eventually realises he has no choice. When they get to Egypt, Joseph calls the brothers, including Simeon, into his palace. They are terrified but he offers them a meal and sends them on their way with food. He also adds one final twist: a silver cup in Benjamin's bag. Soon after they've left, Joseph has them chased and brought back. The 'theft' is revealed and the brothers are devastated, especially Judah, who has promised his father that he will look after Benjamin, come what may.

So Judah makes Joseph an offer. 'Do anything you want with me,' he says, 'but spare Benjamin, for it will kill our poor father to lose him. Take my life instead of his.'

Joseph can keep up the pretence no longer and he tells his brothers who he is. That makes them even more scared, but this story is about mercy, not revenge; it's about bad things being turned to good, not good things going bad. So Jacob goes to see his lost son, Joseph, and they all settle in Egypt. Jacob can't quite believe what's happened. It's almost as if it's a dream, which is, of course, how things started in this family.

After Jacob's death, Joseph's brothers think he'll take his revenge. But Joseph has learned that things can work for good with God if we let them. So there are no more fights or wars or murders or scandals but simply a period of living quietly with the promise that one day God will lead the family back home. Given the troubles along the way, that's what you call a result.

Genesis in short

Good and bad, light and dark, the start of learning about each other and about the creator. The place to realise that God will stick by people even when they don't necessarily deserve it. Journeys, squabbles, falling out with each other. A book which shows that what is broken can be mended. At its heart, the discovery that sacrifice isn't about how much or what is given but how we spend our lives for those who need us.

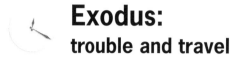

Exodus:
trouble and travel

The first five books of the Bible are called the Pentateuch. It simply means five scrolls or five books. They're known as the Moses books and he is very much centre stage here. In Exodus you get history, law and worship all together in what becomes a long and winding road to freedom.

Exodus is a story about people stepping out and making a new start. You wouldn't guess it, mind you, from the number of complaints. It's about freedom and God leading the way for arguably the most reluctant followers in the whole of history.

It begins 400 years after Joseph's dreams. The Hebrews are still in Egypt but now they are no longer partners. Instead, they are slaves. They're also a threat, a growing minority who could side with enemies in wartime. The government solution is simple and brutal: kill the baby boys.

Many die, but one beautiful child is hidden by his mother and, when he's too big to be hidden, he's left in a place where the princess comes to bathe. The baby's sister, Miriam, has placed herself close by. The princess finds the child and decides to take care of him. Miriam appears, saying, 'I can find a nurse for you,' and it ends up with mum looking after her own baby, while being paid by the king's daughter to do it. Success in almost anybody's books!

The princess names him Moses: the special one. He grows up in the palace but doesn't forget his roots. As a young man, he sees a slave master beating up one of his countrymen. He can't help but get involved. In the ensuing fight, Moses kills the slave master and has to flee in order to save his own life.

Back into trouble

Over the border, in Midian, Moses gets a job with Jethro looking after sheep. Quiet years follow when nothing out of the ordinary happens but, one day, all that changes. Moses sees a bush on fire. Not exactly a shock in the desert – but this one isn't burning out. He gets a bit closer.

'Near enough,' says a massive voice. 'Shoes off, this is holy ground.' God tells Moses about the suffering of the Hebrews in Egypt. 'I have heard them and I will rescue them… with you as leader.'

'Me?' says Moses.

'I'll be with you,' replies God.

'And, er, who will I say has sent me?'

'I am who I am' – this is God, no further explanation needed.

Moses is not exactly enthusiastic. In fact, he tries several times to refuse the job. God gives him signs of his power, including a walking stick that turns into a snake and back again. Aaron, his brother, becomes his diplomatic support.

'Now,' says God, 'get out there and do it.'

When the two of them arrive in Egypt, Moses impresses the Hebrews and gets commissioned to negotiate with Pharaoh about time off for the Hebrew slaves. Pharaoh is stunned… but not in a good way.

'Let's get this straight,' he says. 'You want me to give slaves a three-day break for some sort of religious holiday? I clearly need to give them more work to do.'

Suddenly, the idea of Moses as their leader doesn't seem so wonderful to the Hebrews. He's just made their lives even more impossible. Moses complains to God that it's all gone wrong. 'Patience,' says God. 'Watch and wait.'

A speech to rally people's spirits is a disaster and the walking stick which turns into a snake leaves Pharaoh unimpressed. 'Let my people go' is God's command to Egypt's leader and it's backed by the first of ten plagues – the River Nile turned to blood.

Pharaoh can ignore this by retreating to his palace, but a frog infestation is different. He decides to make a deal with Moses… which he cancels the moment the frogs are gone.

Plague three is gnats, four is flies, five is dead animals and six is boils. You'd think the king would be getting the message by now. It's the storm of the century next: huge hailstones, flattening crops and killing anyone still out in the fields. 'Enough,' he says. 'I have sinned and I will let you all go.'

'I don't believe you,' says Moses, and he's right.

A locust alert fails to rattle Pharaoh, but the rest of the government are getting seriously worried. 'This is a disaster,' they tell him. 'Just let them go.'

After locusts, it is darkness, so black you can't even see your hand in front of you. Pharaoh meets Moses but nothing gets sorted. Then the final plague: the death of all first-born sons.

On the night it happens, the Hebrews have a family meal of roast lamb and flatbread, a sort of early kebab. This is the night when the Angel of Death passes over the Hebrew houses, but knocks on each Egyptian door, including Pharoah's.

'Leave us and take all you have with you,' Pharaoh tells Moses as he faces the horror of his own son's death, 'but ask your God to be kind to me.'

On the road again

The Hebrew exit route looks odd; it's certainly not the quickest, but it has a purpose. They're taking a route from which there can be no going back. It's the big-change journey as slaves become a nation again.

When Pharaoh realises the problems of having no labour force, he changes his mind yet again and mobilises the army. The Hebrews are by the Red Sea when the Egyptians appear on the horizon.

'Well, that's just great,' the Hebrews tell Moses. 'You drag us away from slavery so we can be slaughtered here! Why couldn't you have left us where we were?'

Moses declares that the Lord will help them, and the Lord says: 'Why do you keep calling out? Just move forward.'

So they do. Moses uses his stick again and east winds create a path through the sea. They get across, but the Egyptian army gets stuck, and the returning waters finish them off.

At last, the people seem to realise just how great a God they have and they compose a song of praise to him. But the good mood doesn't last. There's a never-ending hunt for water, and food is not exactly plentiful. That's when the people go back to what they're best at: moaning and talking about the 'good old days'.

In spite of the whingeing, God orders a roast quail feast for them, followed by a regular bread delivery. It's actually manna rather than bread: white, flaky, a bit like honey biscuits. Even then, their trust in God never lasts longer than the next problem.

Plenty happens during their desert journey. There's water to be found, battles to be won, disputes to be resolved. Moses is joined by the rest of his family, and his father-in-law teaches him that he can't do everything himself. A series of leaders are appointed so that everyone has someone to turn to.

What to do and how not to do it

At Mount Sinai, God calls Moses to him. There's smoke, thunder, lightning and Moses receives some basic guidelines for the people – the ten commandments:

1 God comes first... always.
2 No substitutes for God, no alternative focus.
3 Take care to use God's name wisely and well.
4 One rest day every seven: take a break.
5 Treat your parents with respect.
6 No killing.
7 No adultery.
8 No thieving.
9 No lying.
10 No wanting what someone else has got and you haven't.

This isn't the end of the rules by any means. There are another three chapters of them, ranging from how to cook goat to what to do with your enemy's donkey. The heart of the matter, though, can be summed up in nine words: be fair, be responsible, stick with the real God. The section finishes with a promise from the people not just to hear the rules but to follow them faithfully.

Then it's the arrangements for worship in mind-boggling detail. Everything required for their worship space is specified – from the big tent to the massive alfresco courtyard. And, at its heart, is the Covenant Chest which represents the promises that bind God and his people together.

Priests are chosen and there's a ceremony of forgiveness – because everyone needs that, even leaders. There's information about sacrifices, incense, oils and how to pay for the upkeep of all this. It sounds as if everything's in place, especially when God says: 'I will live among you and you will remember how I rescued you.'

However, nothing stays sorted for long in this story, and one day when Moses doesn't return quickly enough from meeting God on the mountain, the people get Aaron to make a golden bull to protect them. Then they celebrate by getting very, very drunk.

God feels frustrated enough to think about starting again somewhere different. Moses is so angry that he breaks the stones on which the rules are written and the episode ends in disease and death.

It's not quite the same after that, but it's not the end. God still goes on caring for his messed-up, messy people, even if their behaviour would be enough to drive anyone to distraction. When Moses needs him, God is still there to talk to. And there's a second set of the stones with the rules on, a mark that God's promise is constant even if his people aren't.

It's followed by reminders about particular rules, and the book draws to a close by going over some of the details of worship. It shows that people wanted to get the details right but getting things to look perfect isn't the heart of faith.

What matters is God being there: forgiving them, leading them and, for once, seeing them follow. Exodus: the book of stepping out, going forward, moving on.

Thoughts on God from Exodus

- When he calls you, listen.
- When he sends you, he also equips you.
- When he's with you, that doesn't mean instant success.
- When life isn't working out, keep faith.

Leviticus:
the priest book

This is basically a handbook with some 300 rules for the people in charge of the Jewish religion 3,000 years ago. So it's not a novel in a list of *50 Best Beach Reads*; it's more like a manual to dip into, a way of trying to see that things run smoothly.

The promise that underpins Leviticus is clear. 'I will walk with you,' God promises in chapter 26. The rules that come before the promise are designed to help people to be his people.

That doesn't explain why the book starts with sacrificing goats and bulls on bronze altars. To understand that, you need to look at chapter 20 where you realise that it's a time when people were killing their own children to please pagan gods. Not here, God tells them, not now or ever. If you want to sacrifice something, it must not be another human life.

In fact, Leviticus makes clear there are lots of things you *can* sacrifice: grain, animals, flour, baked bread, yeast, honey and salt. They're all good so long as you're offering the best and doing it with love and care. If you bring along second-rate stuff, it shows you don't really mean it: you're not sorry for what you've done; you're not thankful for what you've got.

That takes us to sin, the thing that separates us from God. Sometimes sin can occur without people even realising properly that it's occurred. There's no sense in saying, 'I wasn't ready.' It's done. It can also be one of those things that the whole world seems to be doing, which also isn't an excuse. And anyone, from the top to the bottom, can find themselves involved. In short, it happens.

Sacrifice is the sign that you want to put things straight. But it's not a competition. If you can't afford a lamb, then doves or pigeons are just as good. If you can't even pay for a pigeon, simply bring your best flour. Whatever you are able to do, that's fine with God.

The devil isn't always in the detail

If you happen to like details, this is the place to find them. You want to make an offering for a blessing? Make sure the priest gets the upper joint of the right hind leg of the animal. Leviticus always lets you know where you are.

If I say burn the bread on the altar, God tells them, none of it must be eaten. If I set down a rule, that's what I mean.

It may well sound this fierce because people always seem to be taking liberties. Take chapter 6 and the sin of cheating. The writer makes sure you know what God means. Keeping back some of the stuff that you were just storing for a friend is cheating. Finding something that isn't yours and saying nothing about it is cheating. It doesn't matter how you bend the rules, the fact is that you do. So this book says it in words of one syllable: don't do it.

It also describes how Aaron and his family became priests, including all the details about his coat, sash, belt and gold hat. The gold is a reminder that God's in charge, not us. If you're keen on status, God isn't for you.

What to do is written down in detail so all you have to do is follow it. Two of Aaron's sons do that and two don't. 'Let's experiment' might have been what Nadab and Abihu were thinking. 'Let's push the boundaries.' So they do. They burn incense where they shouldn't and land up burnt to death themselves. Aaron doesn't know what to say, so it's Moses who explains that people in positions of power ignore the rules at their own peril.

Health, sex and happiness

Then there's a pile of lifestyle advice for nomadic people in a hot country. No place round here, says God, for eating camels or badgers or eagles or bats or sea gulls… and don't even think about touching moles, rats, mice or lizards. If you're hungry, fish is fine but so are locusts and grasshoppers – not so attractive.

This is followed by the arrangements for keeping people in isolation when they've got infectious diseases. Not very sociable, but then there are no antibiotics on tap here. On the good news side, there's reassurance that going bald isn't an illness.

Not everything is medicine and misery. They start a summer festival, a Great Day of Forgiveness: it's a holiday, a break, a place to start again.

A few more details and then sex gets some serious attention. Don't do what other people do, just because everyone else is doing it, God explains. Remember that I want you to be different from those around you. The advice is basically very simple: love the one you've chosen to be with. And if anyone is in doubt about what God means there's a list of 19 eye-watering examples of bad practice.

After that, there's an assortment of rules ranging from respect for your parents to how to look after new fruit trees. Here are a few of them:

- Pay what you owe the moment it's due.
- Don't make fun of someone who's got a disability.
- Don't let anger get a hold of you.
- Don't hold grudges.
- If you get the chance, speak up for someone in trouble.

And, in the middle of these rules, the best advice of all: love others as much as you love yourselves.

Punishment, celebration and perfection

The rules are followed by the punishments. Not pleasant, but then some of the things people got up to weren't very pleasant either. If it's any consolation, the rules for ordinary people are far simpler than the ones for those in charge. There are arrangements for the big annual festivals plus reminders that, wherever you are, you need a rest day once a week, from the greatest to the least.

There are repetitions such as the very obvious warning that, if an animal just drops dead, it's probably not a good idea to cook it for dinner. And, towards the end, there's the Year of Jubilee which starts on the Great Day of Forgiveness once every 50 years. This is when all debts are cancelled and the people remember anew that everything they have comes from God.

Even in the regular years, there are special arrangements for those who are poor. You don't take advantage of them; you treat people as people, not as property. Equally, you must be fair to those who are rich. Do right by me and I'll do right by you, God tells them. And don't make promises you can't keep.

The book finishes with a list of offerings and regulations, but this rule book isn't really just a list of rules. At the heart of it is God – the one who is different. 'I'm not like the other gods around you,' he tells his people, 'and I don't want you to be like the other people around you. Do things with care, do things well, but don't get so hung up on perfection that you fail to look after each other.' As Leviticus says and Jesus reminds people: love others just as much as you love yourselves.

The essence of Leviticus

God walks with us, holds us when we are sorry and accepts what we are able to give, however great or small. No one needs to look over their shoulder at what someone else can bring or do. Stay safe; stay healthy; treat each other well. And let the rules guide you, not strangle you.

Numbers:
doing detail, getting sorted

If Leviticus is a sort of handbook, Numbers is a kind of journal. It's written for people scratching around in the desert for a living while looking for a land of their own. A curious mixture of poetry, songs, prayers, prophecy, laws… and a walking stick that produces almonds. Plus, for those who enjoy such things, loads of lists and plenty of numbers.

Welcome to organisation in its infinite variety: plans for camping, rules for infectious diseases, a 'who-does-what' for priests – pretty much everything gets covered. One moment it's criminal damage laws and a page or two later it's haircut regulations.

Worship planning includes six strong carts and twelve oxen. This is a music and prayer festival that goes wherever they go. The contract details for the job of priest come next, along with the good news that, if you get chosen, you don't start work till the age of 25 and you retire at 50.

The arrangements for worship also recognise that there can be circumstances which don't fit the rules and that God is happy to make exceptions where necessary. Even more important, he's delighted to include all people, wherever they come from.

The daily muttering

This is a nation on the move, so you get travel details served with a bonus portion of complaints: 'In Egypt, we could eat melons and cucumber and fish and meat. What do we get now? Manna followed by manna followed by manna.'

'Lord,' says Moses to God, 'what have I done to deserve this bunch of grumblers? It's too much. If this is all you've got planned for me, finish me off now.'

Not a great prayer!

'Find 70 reliable leaders for me,' says God. A problem shared, you see, is a problem halved… or, indeed, divided by 70. As for meat, the Lord tells him, get the people ready to eat so much that, by the end of the month, they'll utterly sick of it. Moses is unconvinced but, in the blink of an eye, the sky is filled with birds and roast quail season has arrived.

When the 70 leaders are commissioned, two start to prophesy. Joshua is shocked. 'Surely, that's your job,' he tells Moses.

'Don't worry about my status,' Moses replies. 'I'd be happy if God's Spirit filled everyone like that.'

A search party checks out Canaan. Spies report that the food is fabulous and the fields are fertile, but the people who are already there look quite strong. The Israelites promptly start saying it's a land of giants where nothing grows: the art of making the challenging sound impossible so you don't have to do anything difficult.

This is not a comfortable read. The cost of fear is more long years in the desert and the cost of outright defiance is death. But, for those who stumble and want to get back up on their feet, this is the God of second chances.

The bad times create mutterings plus further nostalgia for the food in Egypt. 'There, we had grapes and figs and pomegranates,' the people sigh, 'and here we don't even have water.' Moses solves this problem by making water rush out from a rock he hits with his stick. In spite of this, the place becomes known not as the site of a miracle but instead as the place where they moaned to God.

Don't be an ass

Nothing comes easily to these folk. Their relatives in Edom refuse to help them. Aaron, who has been Moses' right-hand man, dies. Battles galore have to be fought. To be honest, the Israelites don't look great but they are tough, as King Og discovers when he attacks. Victories mean a place they can stay and a powerful reputation.

Another neighbouring king called Balak is so worried by them that he calls for a magician called Balaam to put a curse on these newcomers. Balaam sends back a thoroughly unexpected answer. 'No deal,' he says, 'they've been blessed by God himself.'

King Balak comes back with a better offer so the magician agrees to meet him. On the way there, his donkey keeps stopping as it sees an angel on the path. Balaam, who can see nothing, gives the beast a good thrashing. Eventually the donkey says: 'Why do you keep beating me?'

'Because you're making me look stupid,' he replies, without appearing to think that talking donkeys are a bit unusual.

Suddenly the angel is visible and reminds Balaam that he's only safe if he's speaking for God. So that's what he does. It puzzles King Balak, who can't work out why Balaam keeps offering blessings to their new neighbours.

Notes for a better tomorrow

With God on their side, you might begin to think the Israelites would get on quietly with their lives. No chance. Some of the men become involved with some of the local women, then with some of the local religions and the resultant mess ends in death and destruction.

When that gets sorted, there's a head count so that everyone can receive a fair share of the land. This includes women, thanks to Mahlah, Noah, Hoglah, Milcah and Tirzah, five sisters who make the case that having somewhere to call home is not just an issue for men. Numbers is radical and clear about fairness: everyone is included, everyone has a place.

The succession to Moses is sorted out. Joshua will deal with the army and Eleazar will look after religious matters: recognition that it's time to do things differently. There's a long list of sacrifices with detail about the ingredients and methods.

Then there's stuff about keeping promises, plus practical information about how it works when people make promises they cannot possibly keep. War, travel, boundaries and inheritance laws are all covered, along with a good deal more.

It's a series of snapshots of a big family as they grow together, a book to take in bit by bit, not a novel to gallop through. Some of it may look primitive and brutal today; some of it seems surprisingly modern. Numbers is strong on fairness and expects people to be organised enough so that talking about what is right can be transformed into actually doing it.

And it has one of the greatest prayers in the world tucked away in its sixth chapter: 'May the Lord bless you and keep you, may he make his face to shine upon you and light up your life with kindness; may he watch over you and give you peace.'

Good news in Numbers

- Wherever people are from, they're welcome with God.
- Problems have solutions, if you bother to seek them.
- Sharing the work makes all things possible.
- Failure isn't the end – there are still second chances.
- God longs to let his face shine upon us.

Deuteronomy:
choose life

The final book of the Moses cycle takes another look back at his life. This is history written in the present tense. Translations don't usually follow that because we think of our yesterdays as the past. Not so, back then. History was seen as if it was living, breathing and making sense of life today.

These are the last words of Moses Rodbearer as he says goodbye to the people he has led for 40 years. They are about to cross the Jordan to the promised land but his time is now over. So this final chapter of his life starts with five messages linked to the people's story:

- You've been here long enough; it's time to move on.
- Choose your leaders wisely and be fair to each other.
- Don't moan, don't worry, just trust God.
- Disobedience is expensive and painful.
- If you stick with God – the one God – good things happen.

Moses tells them how special they are: nothing like this has ever happened before; no one else has heard God speak as you have; no one else has known God's love as you have; no one else has seen his power as you have. So get to know your history and get to know your God.

The power of ten

The second speech is the long one and includes a repeat of the ten basic rules:

1 God comes first… always.
2 No substitutes for God, no alternative focus.
3 Take care to use God's name wisely and well.
4 One rest day every seven: take a break.
5 Treat your parents with respect.
6 No killing.
7 No adultery.
8 No thieving.
9 No lying.
10 No wanting what someone else has got and you haven't.

Moses reminds the people how they had a sense of God's greatness and power when these rules were given. That's great… but what matters most, says Moses, is that you obey them.

In case anyone finds ten a bit of a stretch on the memory, there's an even shorter version: a top two. First, you need to know that there is only one true God. Nice and simple really. Second, you need to love that God with all your heart, all your soul, all your strength.

And, if you find rules hard to remember, keep working at it. Say them aloud at home, repeat them when you're out walking, write them up on doors and gates. Whatever works for you, do it.

Responsibility can be terrifying

There's a promise of good things to come, but also a warning of how easily people drift when they've got what they want. Then there's a note that children depend on what they see in adults. Terrifying! The instructions regarding war are uncompromising and sound brutal. The reason is fear they'll dilute their beliefs with other people's ideas and what has made them special will be lost.

If the people keep their identity, they're promised a land where they need never be hungry again, a place with everything they could possibly need. It's not because they deserve it but because God is merciful. Respect him, love him, serve him. And put your heart and soul into it.

In a time of a thousand and one gods, Moses explains that theirs is unique. This is the Lord of the heavens and the earth: his power is awesome, but he uses it fairly. He doesn't do bribery and corruption, but he does care big-time for those who can't look after themselves. He treats you as special, but he loves those you think of as foreign, too. In short, he's God for everyone, everywhere.

The older people are told they have a special responsibility: the more you've seen, the more it's up to you to set a good example. Farmers are offered a place where the weather will do most of the hard work for them.

Then everyone is asked to decide between a blessing in a land of promises or a curse as they drift through the years behaving like everybody else. It sounds like the easiest choice in the universe, but the desire to fit in with the people around them is terrifyingly strong. God lays down ground rules in detail and with a passion. Disobedience will mean death.

From vultures to grapevines

The food arrangements are clear. Lamb, beef and fish get the seal of approval but camels, vultures, bats and screech owls are off the menu. The ten per cent rule for sharing is set out with a reminder that this isn't just for God or the church but also for those in need: strangers, widows, orphans. There are arrangements for not letting debt be a burden forever and for slaves to be made free.

The rules in this book cover all sorts of situations: unsolved murders, beautiful female prisoners, roof safety and tassel-wearing. Deuteronomy does detail without worrying too much about what comes next: outdoor toilets, interest rates and saying what you mean follow quickly one after another.

The justice system gets directions about evidence and how to deal with those who lie in court. The army regulations take the liberal approach to human rights close to an all-time high. You don't have to fight if:

- you're engaged to be married
- you've just built a house
- you've just planted grapevines
- you're scared.

And, for the overenthusiastic soldier, there's a reminder that fruit trees are *not* the enemy.

Giving special attention to those in need gets several mentions. If someone is poor, pay them first, says Moses. And don't take advantage of those who haven't got a father or are away from home; remember that in the past you needed help, too. This isn't about rules in a vacuum; it's about keeping a people together and never forgetting how they came to be where they are.

Saying means doing

There's a ceremony of blessings and curses with everyone yelling 'Amen!' in the right places. The message is simple. Doing good can lead to more good things; choosing what is wrong only leads to the place where life falls apart.

Moses challenges people to be real with God. Don't think to yourself: I'll say the right things but go my own way. Take God's path and, even if things are hard for a while, he'll bring you back together again. No one's being called to do the miraculous or impossible. Will you love God and walk his roads or will you take your heart elsewhere? It's up to you but it's a life-and-death decision. Choose life.

Joshua, the new leader, is told not to get discouraged. Then, the history and the law books are passed on… but with a sad anticipation that the rules will be forgotten once they settle in their comfortable new place.

Moses ends with a song of love and betrayal that warns his people about what could happen if they forget the story of their lives together. Take it to heart, Moses tells them, and live long in the land.

Finally he blesses each and every one of them, then climbs the mountain to glimpse the promised land before he dies. The book finishes with a blessing: a prayer about the God of the sunrises, the God of the harvests, the God of every good gift. So Moses leaves them with one more river to cross and the message that God doesn't call you to stand still but to move on.

The heart of Deuteronomy

Moving on but remembering where you came from – that's the essence of Deuteronomy. Knowing that God is great is a start, but it means nothing if you don't follow what he says. There's a choice: blessings in a land of promises or a world which forgets God and falls apart. The advice is simple: choose life.

Joshua:
renewing the promise

Another title for this book could be 'Life after Moses'. Joshua was one of the twelve who had secretly checked out the land of Canaan where the people hoped to settle. Only he and Caleb had reported that the land was good and the task possible. This is where Joshua gets the chance to match his words with actions.

A new leader, a move to the other side of the River Jordan, a bit of settling down: the basics of this book are simple enough. Joshua promises to do what God requires and the people promise to follow him. What could possibly go wrong?

Spies take a close look at the land ahead and are helped by Rahab, who lives by Jericho's city wall. Joshua explains that the Covenant Chest with the ten commandments in it will go ahead of them and all they have to do is follow.

The moment comes and, when the box hits the river, the waters back off and the nation crosses safely, just like the Red Sea all those years before. The people take twelve stones from the river to remind them how God gave them a new land and Joshua led them into it.

Battling it out

After the river comes the city: Jericho. The people there lock the gates and get ready for a long fight. Instead of a blood-curdling attack, they hear seven horns playing quietly and see people marching round the walls in silence. Weird!

Six days pass like this. On the seventh, there's an almighty blast on those horns, a shout and the walls fall down. Jericho becomes victory number one.

The city of Ai should be next on the list. The advance party report that it's not so large: an easier task with fewer soldiers required. It goes terribly wrong and, in the shame of failure, Joshua blames it all on God just like Moses used to.

'Why have you brought us here?' he demands. 'We were okay on the other side of the river. Now, we're completely wrecked and our enemies will kill us!'

God explains that the people can't defeat their enemies because they're not wholeheartedly on board with his plans for them. The finger of guilt points at Achan, who admits to theft back in Jericho: gold, some silver and a fabulous coat all the way from Babylon. Joshua can't quite believe that someone would value these things above God. After the city of Ai is finally taken, there's a ceremony to remind everyone of their promises.

The new start lasts no longer than the blink of an eye. The Jews make a treaty with the people of Gibeon without a moment's thought about what God might say. Then they pray for approval once they have already made their mind up. Wrong way round.

Much of the time, this is a book of blood-curdling battles, so it's not ideal reading for a summer picnic. But it was a world where human sacrifice and temple prostitution were commonplace. God is clear – his people can't just be like everyone else.

Sorting it out

By now, Joshua is getting old. Instead of a retirement package, he gets more stuff to sort out. Number one on that list is to get the land properly allocated so that everyone has somewhere to live: 6,000 words listing weird names and strange places. But detail matters if you want things to be right.

That's followed by arrangements to stop revenge killings running out of control and the allocation of where the priests will live. The result is people settled peacefully. There's a good feeling in the land because God has kept his promises – every one of them.

The feeling doesn't last. Next, there's a furious row over a new altar, with people outraged, appalled and disgusted… until they actually bother to speak to each other. Then the ones who wanted a fight in order to maintain traditional standards discover they've completely misunderstood what's going on. Talking together seems to make a good starting point for life together.

The choice

Time passes quietly and Joshua's life draws to a close. 'I've tried to sort out what I can for our new land,' he tells them. 'Don't forget there's much more to come if you can follow the rules and avoid the bad behaviour you'll sometimes see around you. Remember how God chose Abraham and gave him a family; how he used Moses to unlock the doors of slavery; how he brought us through the desert and the battles to a land where life is good. Will you cling to your old ways and do what everyone else does, or will you follow God?'

The people say yes, of course they'll follow God, but Joshua isn't convinced. Still they keep on declaring that they're ready for the challenge.

'Well,' he tells them, 'then you are my witnesses. But, seeing that you're so keen, you need to throw out the alternatives to God you've got tucked away just in case.' The people go on yelling for God and Joshua renews the promise. A stone under an oak tree marks the place.

The book never tells you directly what Joshua thought and felt in those last days, but he seems like someone who knows there's a lot more to life than shouting God's name enthusiastically when you're trying to keep promises.

Basics about life from Joshua

- To sort out things fairly so that everyone has a home is the heart of life together.

- Try not to start an argument before you know what you're arguing about.

- If you're going to follow, you have to let God lead.

Home
Exile
Love
Faith
Home

Home
Exile
Love
Faith
Home

Home
Exile
Love
Faith
Home

Home
Exile
Love
Faith
Home

Judges:
could do better

So who or what are Judges? They're military leaders who are also responsible for the law and some worship. An end-of-year report would probably say 'could do better'. When things get tough, their instincts are to compromise, do it their own way and not worry too much about whether it's right or not. This, for better or worse, is their story.

The story of what happens after Joshua dies begins with an enemy king having his thumbs and big toes sliced off. Don't be too shocked. It's punishment for doing the same thing to 70 other people.

As the old generation who had lived through hard times in the desert dies out, so does the memory of what God did for them. The people of God, who were once so different to others, now seem like everyone else.

Great victories are replaced by sad defeats. Good leaders don't last. War is never far away and the details are not for the squeamish. Ehud plunges his sword so far into Eglon's flesh that it gets lost there. Heber's wife, Jael, helps someone hide from his attackers and then drives a tent peg straight through his skull once he's asleep.

Any excuse

In this time of wars, God calls Gideon. It doesn't look like a great decision when the man chosen pitches straight into a complaint: 'If you're supposed to be helping us, Lord, why are we having such a terrible time?'

Then it's excuses and doubts: 'Frankly, I'm useless at this sort of thing. Is it really God speaking? Prove it.' Flames burst out of a rock, burning to a cinder the offering he's supposed to be making. 'Oh no,' he mutters, remembering what he's said so far, 'Now I'm going to die.'

God tells him to calm down: 'You're not going to die. You're simply going to pull down an altar to another god and we're going to start again.' Gideon, brave as ever, works in the dead of night to avoid any unpleasantness.

His next task is to lead the army. Scared silly, he demands ridiculous proof that he should be doing this. 'I'm going to leave a fleece out and I want the morning dew to cover the wool but leave the floor stone-dry.' It works.

Amazing… but not enough for Gideon. He also wants to see it work the other way round: fleece dry, floor soaking wet. The book wisely avoids recording what God is thinking by this stage. But the miracle happens.

Does Gideon lead out his 32,000-strong army and defeat the Midianite enemies? Not quite. Now it's God's turn to test Gideon. 'Send home anyone who's afraid,' he tells him. That's 22,000 gone.

'Still too many,' says God. 'Take them to the springs and watch them drink.' Over 9,000 just lap it up with any nasty parasites that may happen to be in the water; only 300 show a bit more care and scoop water into their hands.

'They're the ones,' God declares. 'Send the rest home… but keep their trumpets.' And Gideon does so.

'Now, I know how scared you are,' God explains, 'so slip down to the enemy camp and listen.'

Hidden in the shadows, Gideon can hear the guards discussing a nightmare, plus their worries about what this man called Gideon can do with God on his side.

That's how it turns out. The trumpets confuse a jumpy enemy and burning torches add to the effect. In the confusion, the Midianites start fighting each other. Victory number one has begun and Gideon just has to finish the job.

The Israelites are impressed enough to want him as king. Not a good idea, he tells them, the focus would then be on me, not God. But he accepts some gold, makes a statue and starts worshipping it. It's the classic Judges two-step: one forward, the next one back.

Bad to worse

With Gideon's death, it gets worse. His son, Abimelech, hires thugs to kill all his brothers. The youngest one, Jotham, escapes and tells the people he's shocked by how they just accept violence. It's no surprise, then, when Abimelech is killed by a woman who drops a massive rock from a great height straight on to his skull.

Tola and Jair are the next leaders, followed by an unusual choice. Jephthah is the result of a meeting between his father and a local prostitute. He's not even wanted by his own family. But he's tough and, when times get hard, that's who the people turn to. As a soldier, he's the best, but he makes a terrible mistake. In a fit of bravado, he tells God that, if he wins a battle, he will burn the first living creature he sees on his return as an offering.

When he comes back home across the river, it's not a goat or sheep he sees. Instead, a child comes singing and dancing to meet her daddy: his only daughter. Not all promises are good promises. Sometimes you should admit how foolish your words were. But Jephthah puts sacrifice above mercy and the story lurches again from triumph to tragedy.

Hair there and everywhere

More leaders come and go; then it's the hairy one. Samson is chosen by God from the beginning. The long hair and the strength in those shoulders are front-page news, but his life often looks like something out of a cheap magazine: a lion ripped apart with his bare hands, burning fox tails and killings by the hundred.

There's also a weakness for women and an inclination to give away secrets. Delilah is offered big money to find out why he's so strong. She doesn't succeed by appealing to love or respect but hits the jackpot by nagging. Samson eventually tells her how he believes his strength comes from the promise to God never to cut his hair.

When the enemy next turn up, Samson realises that his hair has been cut, the Lord has left him and he's trapped. His enemies poke his eyes out and he's put to work pushing a millstone round like a blinded ox.

The end comes when Samson, his strength returning, brings the house down at a holiday festival: a warning of the dangers of putting big blokes next to roof-bearing pillars. It's also a reminder that it's never too late to seek out God.

How to blow it

Micah comes next: a man, in many ways, just as daft as Samson. First, he steals money from his mother. Not a good idea. Then, when she curses the thief, he admits, 'It's me, mum.'

And, in order to uncurse the curse, they turn the stolen silver into… a gift for the poor or something beautiful for God? Absolutely not. They make an idol – the one thing above all others God doesn't want them to do.

Then Micah employs a private priest on the basis that you're probably fine if you've got connections with gods. The priest only stays loyal until someone makes him a better offer.

If you want a list of examples of how not to do it, Judges is the place. Even worse, ordinary people get hurt in the fallout. It's no surprise that the last pages of the book are packed full of violence and its consequences.

Judges sums up the situation in these words: people just did what they liked. Doing your own thing has rarely looked as ugly and dangerous as it does here. If there's one message that runs through all the mess, it's this: don't get carried away by what you say or think or do; concentrate on listening to what God says and thinks and does.

Headlines from Judges

- Being scared is not an excuse for doing nothing.
- God uses all sorts of people so long as they let him.
- Keeping a promise is only good if it's a sensible promise in the first place.
- God puts up with a lot… far more than we do.
- No matter how far you've walked into the darkness, God is still listening for the call that says you want to come back to him.

Ruth:
love's journey

In the middle of the history books in the Old Testament, up pops a love story. It's set at the same time as the book of Judges. Ruth comes from Moab, a country that Israel was often at war with. So, in terms of mixed marriages, the tale of Ruth and Boaz is probably as controversial as it gets. The word 'redemption' occurs 23 times in this small book. It means taking on the cost of saving someone from evil – what true love will always do.

When you get married, you get married for life. At least, that's the idea. Settle down, have a family perhaps and be relatively happy ever after. So it was that Naomi married Elimelech. They had two sons – Mahlon and Chilion. It wasn't perfect. Rarely is. Poor harvests and the need to work took the family from Bethlehem to Moab but they got by and made a life for themselves.

Then, a nasty surprise, because when you say 'till death do us part' you don't expect it to happen any time soon. Elimelech died and left Naomi to cope with two growing lads, which she did… because she had to.

The boys married nice local girls: Orpah and Ruth. Happy ever after again. Except it only lasted about ten years. Two more deaths – sons this time – and three very lonely women.

Now remember that Naomi doesn't come from Moab. She's Bethlehem born and sometimes misses the place, especially when she hears the good times have returned to her country. So she says, 'Now or never. I'm going home.'

Wherever you go

Her daughters-in-law leave with her. That's the tradition. But Naomi worries that it's a daft tradition. 'You're not Bethlehem girls,' she says. 'Return to your own families where you can feel comfortable. You've been good to me, so may God be good to you. After all, you're still young enough to start again, find another man, make another home.'

Because they love Naomi, the goodbyes are full of tears. They tell her how they want to stay with her but she tells them the truth. 'I'm sorry but I can't help you to get married. In fact, I can't help you, full stop. However much I want to.'

Orpah sees the point and bids her mother-in-law a fond farewell. Ruth takes a different line. 'Don't ask me to leave,' she pleads. 'Where you go, I will go; where you live, I will live; your people will be my people; your God will be my God; and, where you die, so will I. Only death will separate me from you.'

Well, what could Naomi say? It wasn't sensible but it was lovely to be cared about so much.

Back home

When they arrive in Bethlehem, there's great excitement. You'd have thought that Naomi would be delighted, but it just makes her loss seem all the worse. 'Don't call me Naomi,' she grumps, 'Call me Mara, because God's made my life bitter. I left with everything; I've come back with nothing.'

That rather spoils the party. On the other hand, there is some truth in it. Naomi and Ruth are broke. Not a penny, not a prospect. That's when you need family and friends.

Now Naomi has a rich relative called Boaz on her husband's side of the family. Depressed, she does nothing about it… or anything else. But Ruth still has a bit of get-up-and-go. 'Let me follow the harvest workers,' she says, 'pick up the bits left behind. I might get real work if they see I'm keen.'

A small kindness

So she goes wherever she can and one of those places belongs to Boaz, not that she knows any-thing about that. As the day wears on, the boss arrives. Boaz spots her almost immediately. 'Who is *that* woman?' he asks his foreman.

'Oh, it's the foreign girl who came with Naomi. She's followed the harvest all day, started really early in the morning.'

Boaz strolls across and invites her to stick with *his* harvest. 'You'll be safe here,' he tells her. 'I've told the men not to take advantage of you. Follow the women and take a drink of water whenever you like.'

Ruth is embarrassed by this small kindness. 'Why should you do this for me? I'm just a foreigner.'

'Not true,' says Boaz with real seriousness. 'You're the one who has been faithful to Naomi way beyond the call of duty. I know what you've done for her. You deserve not only my protection but God's, too.'

It's the gentleness of it all that gets to Ruth. 'Even though I'm no one,' she tells Boaz, 'you've made me feel like someone.'

Mealtime comes and Boaz invites her to eat with them, and to take a share of the leftovers. Then, when it's back to harvesting, he tells his workers to make sure there's plenty left behind for her to gather.

Naomi is stunned when she gets home: 'Ten kilos of corn and free food! That is some field you've found.'

'Belongs to Boaz,' explains Ruth. 'He knows you. Oh, and I can go back whenever I want.'

Love among the barley

The year rolls on and signs of love in the air are… zero. Naomi begins to worry about Ruth again. 'You need a husband, plus you need a place of your own. Listen carefully. It's barley threshing party night over at Boaz's place. Get washed and slip into your posh frock. Then go across and join them. And do nothing until after the eating and drinking.'

Ruth follows Naomi's plan to the letter, snuggling down at the end of the celebrations close to Boaz. The message is unmistakeable and, when Boaz's head clears sometime in the middle of the night, she whispers: 'I want to be yours, I want to marry you.'

Boaz is delighted: 'You could be running after young men right across town but you're not. There is *nothing* I'd like better than to be your husband.'

First, however, he needs the approval of one other family relative. So Ruth goes home, loaded as always with food and this time with a bundle of hope as well.

The end and the beginning

Boaz doesn't waste any time. That morning, he meets the one man who has a prior claim on Naomi's property and daughter-in-law. After talking it through, the man tells Boaz that he'd quite like the land but being responsible for Ruth would be too much for him.

So Boaz buys Naomi and Ruth's freedom, redeeming the land once owned by Elimelech. Having sorted out the legal niceties, Boaz can marry Ruth, which is clearly high on his agenda.

In an age of arranged marriages and family duty, this story pulses with the love of two not-quite-so-young people. The neighbours are just as thrilled as the happy couple. May you be rich, they tell them, may you be famous and have loads of children.

Now, Boaz was already pretty well-off at the start of this tale. As for children and fame, Ruth turns out, in time, to be King David's great-grandmother. And the last picture in the story is Naomi cuddling Ruth's baby boy, redeemed from the bad times by family loyalty and kindness. For once in this world, no one could possibly ask for more.

Ruth – what matters

This book is the reminder that God is for everyone. He's not bothered about what you look like or where you come from but how you behave, how you care for the people you meet. If that means crossing borders, looking for work or returning home without any certainties, sometimes it needs to be done. And it's also the book with the story of how love saves us where we least expect it.

Home
Exile
Love
Faith
Home

Home
Exile
Love
Faith
Home

Home
Exile
Love
Faith
Home

Home
Exile
Love
Faith
Home

1 Samuel:
kingmaker and kings

This is the history of the Jewish people as they move from being a loose grouping of tribes to a single nation, including their desire for a king or queen to lead them. The upside of this wish could be having a person who sets the very best of examples and turns people's hearts and minds towards God. For the downside, just keep reading.

The story begins with Hannah, the childless wife of Elkanah. The couple love each other but the one thing she longs for most hasn't happened. On their annual visit to the temple in the big city, she pours her heart out. Her lips move wordlessly in prayer and there's such passion in it that Eli, the high priest, thinks she's drunk and tells her to sober up.

'I'm not drunk,' she tells him, 'I'm desperate and I've been pouring out my sorrows to the Lord.'

Eli is embarrassed by his mistake: 'Go in peace,' he tells her, 'and may God answer your prayers.'

He does. Samuel, when he's born, is all that Hannah ever wanted. But she also has a sense that this boy belongs to God as much as to her. When he's old enough, she goes back to Eli and suggests that the child might try out as an apprentice in the temple. Samuel takes to the work and grows deeply into the ways of God.

That's more than can be said of Eli's own sons who are, frankly, wasting what they've been given. Eli tells them off, but he doesn't actually do anything. A visiting prophet warns: 'You're letting your sons get away with things as if you love them more than God. That can't continue. The privileges your family has had are almost over.'

The voice you want, the job you don't

Time passes, Eli's sight is fading and Samuel is growing up. One night, he hears a person calling him and runs to Eli. 'You called – I'm here,' he says.

'I didn't. Go to bed,' says the high priest.

It happens again. 'You *did* call me,' insists the youngster.

At the third time of asking, Eli's brain wakes up. It's not me, he explains, God must be calling you. If it happens again, say: 'Speak, Lord, because I'm ready to hear.'

And that's when Samuel gets the sort of job that nobody wants: telling bad news to someone you care about. The message for Eli is about terrible times ahead for him and his family. Samuel probably expects an angry reaction, but Eli is old and the fight has gone from him. 'God must do whatever he thinks is best,' he tells his young helper.

That's almost the end for Eli, but it's only the start for Samuel, who quickly gains a national reputation as someone who knows what God's got to say.

Samuel in charge

These are not easy times. Eli's sons are killed in a battle against the Philistines, who capture the Covenant Chest with God's ten great rules in it. Not that the chest does the Philistines any good. It just seems to bring them trouble and they start passing it around until no city will house it and they send it back.

The Israelites are thrilled by its return but that in itself solves nothing. Samuel tells his people: 'If you really want to put things right, you've got to get rid of the things that get between you and God. Only if you are truly his will rescue be possible.'

We've done it all wrong, they admit, and we want to put it right. It's a turning point. The Philistines are beaten and peace returns. Samuel proves to be a good leader, not just because his focus is on God but because he tries to sort out problems, year by year and town by town. A peace-maker, you see, not just a peace-lover.

But everyone gets old and Samuel is no exception. His sons take over some of the work and, like Eli's boys, they prove to be unreliable, keener on money than God. Perhaps, then, it's no great surprise when the people ask for a king.

Samuel is less than happy but God tells him: 'It's not an alternative to you they want, it's an alternative to me. But they won't like it when they get it, so warn them.'

Samuel is blunt when he speaks. It makes no difference. You know how people are when they get an idea in their head.

Saul at the start

God chooses Saul, a tall, good-looking lad from one of the smaller tribes, and fills him with his Spirit for the work ahead. Mind you, when he's supposed to be stepping forward to take up his job, they find him hiding behind a pile of supplies, suggesting he's as prone to panic as the rest of us.

To be honest, his appointment divides opinion. But the uncertainty lasts only as long as the arrival of the first enemy. The town of Gilead is attacked by Nahash and his army. The people there seek a peace treaty and Nahash agrees… so long as he can gouge everyone's right eye out.

Not a terribly good offer, so the town appeals for help. Saul is ready for battle and tells anyone who isn't that he'll cut their cattle into tiny pieces if they don't join him.

The turn-out is high: Saul delivers a neat military strategy, and he's scattered the enemy by lunchtime. Suddenly, the people then want to kill those who had doubts about him.

'No one will be harmed,' says Saul, 'This is the day the Lord rescued us and we're going to celebrate that.'

After Saul's victory, Samuel looks back at his life so far. 'Let me tell it to you straight,' he warns the people. 'History shows how often you've turned away from God. By asking for a king you've done it yet again. It's the dry season – blue skies from morning to night. Watch, because what's about to happen is God's message.'

In a short while, a cloud can be seen in the distance, then another. Finally, the storm strikes and people are terrified. You don't need to stay afraid, Samuel explains, but you do have to love God with all your heart and not get distracted by everything else in this world.

Skinny kid

King Saul remains a success in battles but he's not good at thinking before he acts. Sometimes it sounds as if he's making it up as he goes along. A new start is called for, so God asks Samuel to find a man to take over when Saul dies. He's sent to Jesse's house where the first son makes a great impression on him.

God sees it differently: the oldest son *looks* the part but it's the heart that matters. Initially, Jesse hasn't even bothered to call his youngest son in from the fields. He's a skinny stick of a kid but handsome and healthy with sparkling eyes. God tells Samuel: that's the one – David.

Back at the palace, a dark spirit is troubling Saul. 'You need music,' his advisors tell him. Their search leads them to David, whose harp-playing soothes the king's heart and mind. In fact, his new musician makes such a difference that David stays.

About this time, the Philistines come up with a giant of a soldier equipped with sword, spear, javelin and massive shield. 'Anybody want to take me on?' roars Goliath. Nobody answers.

In fact, they're so short of volunteer heroes that Saul offers a princess and a life free of all taxes to the man who steps forward and succeeds. Still no takers. Then David says he'll have a go. His brothers think it's ridiculous.

Saul says: 'You… boy? I don't think so.' But David talks him round. The armour that the king provides is useless because David can't even move in it, so he trusts God and puts to use his quick thinking and five stones. It proves to be enough. A single slingshot stuns Goliath and his fall breaks his skull.

Jealous guy

David soon becomes a close friend of Saul's son, Jonathan, but success can lead to jealousy. Saul's good, say the people, but David is twice as good. So the king throws a spear at his harp player. So much for music calming the savage breast!

It's the start of a time where everything Saul does is designed to get David killed. Instead, David keeps succeeding and the problems go on growing. Even Jonathan, who sees the best in people, eventually has to admit that his father is intent on murder, and so he helps his best friend to escape.

It's difficult to become invisible when you're as well-known as David, and people still seek him out as their leader. Saul keeps hunting for his ex-harp player in a deadly game of hide-and-seek among the desert caves.

When the chance of a killer blow arrives, it falls to David. Saul is in a cave, taking a break, and David is hiding right behind him. Instead of finishing him off, he silently cuts off a slice of Saul's coat.

When David steps out of the shadows, Saul is ashamed: 'You've been so good to me while I've been nothing but trouble to you.' It's not exactly a peace treaty but it is a temporary truce.

Samuel's death, soon after, brings everyone together, but David's home remains in the wilderness country. He's a tough, intelligent soldier with a small army. Saul comes hunting him again and David slips into his camp by night. He steals the king's spear but spares his life. Once again Saul is ashamed, but David is unconvinced that the old king can be trusted and draws even further away from the man he once made music for.

The dark end of the street

Saul looks like a lost cause. He summons up the spirit of Samuel from the dead, only to be told of his own doom. In battle, he sees his own sons die before falling on his sword to avoid capture. His enemies take his head and nail his body to the city wall: a dark end to a life that once shone so brightly. But it leaves a land safe at last for David, now a battle-hardened, fair-minded general who ensures that what is won is shared.

A book that started with the desperate prayers of a woman for a child ends with the prospect of a new king and a new start. But this is only part one. Somehow, you guess it isn't going to be that straightforward.

Perspectives in 1 Samuel

This is a story where life is fine when people love God wholeheartedly. At other moments, laziness, jealousy or just avoiding what needs to be done takes over. Samuel discovers you can hear God clearly if you listen carefully. The choice of David as king shows that what you look like matters far less than who you are deep down. And throughout the story, there are right ways and darker roads. As Samuel reminds the people, they have a choice to make.

2 Samuel:
rise and fall

The book of Samuel was too large to fit on one scroll, a long roll normally made of parchment or papyrus. Instead, it came in two parts, like Kings and Chronicles. This second section of Samuel is essentially the story of King David's reign with all its highs and lows.

It's hot in the afternoon sun. Winter has passed and people hunt out a cooler breeze wherever they can. That's what takes the king to the rooftop terrace of his palace. He stretches out, turns and catches a glimpse of a young woman bathing. She has no idea she's being overlooked; he has no idea who she is. From that moment, everything changes.

The story doesn't start there, mind you. Act one, scene one is an out-of-the-way army base. Enter one dust-covered soldier with his clothes in shreds. The message is that Saul, the king and his son Jonathan are dead. The crown now belongs to David. The new king grieves not only for Jonathan, the best friend anyone could ever have, but also for Saul who has fallen so far.

At first, David stays in the wilderness country: just because some people are saying it's safe doesn't mean it is. After a while, he asks God if it's time to return. 'You may set up your home in Hebron,' God tells him. And it's there that he's crowned king.

While David rules in Judah, one of Saul's sons rules in Israel. It's not only a divided kingdom, but it's also a land of battles and murders. Bit by bit, David gains the upper hand. He's seen as the right man – God's choice – and, seven years after being crowned in Hebron, he becomes king of the whole land.

Jerusalem falls to him in an attack along the underground water tunnels of the city and that's followed by a thorough defeat of the Philistines. Things are so secure that the Covenant Chest with the ten commandments can be brought to Jerusalem. As it arrives, David is singing and dancing with the best of them. 'You look like an idiot,' says one of his wives, who clearly thinks it's his job to look respectable.

'I'll dance for God,' he tells her, 'and I'll dance for the joy of what's happened to me. You may think I look stupid but others won't.'

Too comfortable?

So David settles down comfortably in the city. However, like so many people who are given good things, he feels guilty about it. 'Here I am, living in a fine cedar-wood palace,' he tells the prophet, Nathan, 'and the Covenant Chest is still in a tent.'

'Well, do something about it,' the prophet replies.

Wrong advice… and a warning about the need to pray before you speak. God tells Nathan: 'I've always travelled with my people – that's what the chest and its tent are all about. Yes, it's time to settle down, but the job of building something more permanent will be for the next generation.'

The good news for David is that his son will be the one doing the job and the family line will continue throughout history. The king's prayer says it all: 'You're great, God, not me. What more can I say? Nothing and no one matches you. So bless us and our future.'

The section on battles that follows is not for the faint-hearted, but David is more than a good fighter; he's fair and treats people properly. He even looks after Saul's grandson, who is crippled in both feet. In fact, David seems to be one of those people you can always rely on.

One look too many

But everyone has a weakness, which takes us back to that scene in springtime. Someone else is leading David's army, the weather's fine and the king, from his roof garden, spots a young woman bathing. He thinks: 'Who *is* that girl?'

The answer is Bathsheba and she's married to Uriah, one of his army officers. Instead of saying, 'Forget it,' David takes her to his bed. Bathsheba falls pregnant and David calls Uriah back from the front line of battle in order to cover up who the actual father is.

It doesn't work, so the king takes a further step down dark roads. When Uriah goes back to his army duties, he returns to his death: David has fixed the battle plan to get him eliminated.

The king can now place his relationship with Bathsheba on a proper footing by marrying her. Of course, all the ceremonies in the world don't put right a wrong.

The prophet Nathan tells the king a story about how a poor man's lamb was stolen by a rich man who had far more than he needed to start with. David is outraged… then realises he's the man and the theft is not of a lamb but a wife.

Family at war

The king seeks and receives forgiveness but things are never quite the same. Bathsheba's baby boy becomes ill and dies. Next, Amnon, one of David's sons, rapes his half-sister. Absalom, another of David's sons, tells her to keep quiet, waits his time and has Amnon killed at a family party. Then he flees for his life. It's like watching a particularly vicious soap opera, except that this is real.

David mourns Amnon but soon finds he's missing Absalom. His army chief, Joab, arranges a bit of street theatre about a family at war. David thinks the story is genuine and promises to find a solution.

'Then do the same for your own family,' he's told. 'We all die – like water spilt on the ground that cannot be gathered up again. There is no way back from death but there is from exile for your son.'

So Absalom returns and, in time, is reconciled with his father. It sounds like good news and it would be… except Absalom is planning rebellion. He sympathises with anyone who has a complaint and promises them whatever they want. Of course, that's what you can do when you're not in charge.

The rebellion starts in Hebron and David decides he lacks the power to hold Jerusalem. He retreats to the River Jordan and leaves the city to Absalom. Much of the fight seems to have been knocked out of him by the knowledge that his own son wants to kill him.

However, he's wily enough to set up Hushai as a double agent in Absalom's camp. The result is an unexpected victory and Absalom's death. You'd think the king would be delighted or, at least, relieved. But this is his son, and he can think of nothing but his loss.

That doesn't go down well with the army and he has to be reminded of his duties to all his people. He responds with kindness, mercy and generosity, while also enduring squabbles over who has the greatest claim on him.

It's not the end of the troubles. There's another rebellion, a famine, and more battles against the Philistines, including success at a place with the unforgettable name of Gob.

Final thoughts

One of the king's victory poems is used to help wrap up the book. It's David declaring that God is his protection. City walls, good commanders and tough soldiers all play a part, but it is God who saves him and keeps him safe.

'The waves of death and destruction crashed over me,' he says, 'But when I called out in my troubles, he heard me.'

The book has two postscripts: a list of David's best-known soldiers and a strange story about a census that led to an epidemic. But the main story ends with David's final thoughts, including this one: 'A leader who is fair and follows God is like the sun that dawns on a cloudless day and makes the grass sparkle after the rain.' Tomorrow isn't secured by the power of swords and shields, but because God promises that there will be a future.

Perspectives in 2 Samuel

Battles, divisions, rebellions. Joy, dancing and unnecessary guilt about being fortunate. Second Samuel has every aspect of David's reign. There's kindness, fairness and terrible cruelty, all as part of one person's story. It is history mixed with soap opera, prayer and poetry. Above all, there is God who hears and answers when a broken heart calls out in the depths of despair.

1 Kings:
notes from exile

The two-part book of Kings was probably written when God's people were in exile in Babylon. It's the story of the kings of Israel and Judah, all the way from Solomon to the collapse of the kingdoms. It includes fabulous buildings and foolish behaviour.

How did it start so well and still end up in a mess? That's what the two-part book of Kings sets out to explain for people who have ended up as slave labour in a strange land. It begins with a succession issue.

King David's son, Adonijah, thinks he'll be the new king because his father has never denied him anything. When he starts acting as if he's the chosen one, David confirms that the crown is promised to another son, Solomon. As death creeps closer, David offers his final advice to Solomon: obey the rules, keep the faith… and eliminate a few people.

Wise guy

Of course, power is no good if you don't know what to do with it. So when God asks Solomon what he would really like, he says: 'Wisdom – I want to be able to see how things actually are in order to make the right decisions.' God reckons that's a good choice and, because Solomon hasn't asked for wealth, he adds that as a bonus.

The young king soon gets a test of his new skills in an argument about who is the real mother of a baby. Two young women claim the child, but the young king finds the truth in a test of their love for the baby. It's not just what you say but what you do that proves who you are. People are stunned. From here on, it's respect for the new leader because of the skills God has given him.

Solomon's team all get a mention and the population booms. These are the good times, summed up in seven words: they ate, they drank, they were happy. Solomon's ability to get to the heart of things becomes legendary. Famous, wealthy and blessed with peace, he negotiates with King Hiram to source the wood for the long-promised temple.

Big ideas

This is building on a massive scale and perhaps it's where Solomon's big ideas start to get in the way of his wisdom. He drafts in 30,000 of his own people as forced labourers. It's a move that will eventually break the kingdom in two. This is a well-organised and stylish building but God isn't concentrating on the cedar panels, however impressive they may be. Instead, he says: 'If you follow me, I will never abandon you.'

After the temple comes the palace, which takes 13 years to build. It has a main room so big you'd be hard-pressed to see who was at the far end. Not cosy, but spacious.

Eventually, the Covenant Chest with God's ten great rules is installed in the new temple and the whole place suddenly fills with light brighter than a thousand stars – God doesn't just like being there, he loves it. 'This place is for you, Lord,' says Solomon, 'now and forever.'

Deep down, Solomon knows that no building, however grand, can encompass God himself, so he prays simply that their temple will be a place of justice, repentance and forgiveness.

God's response is an encouragement and a warning: 'If you go on serving me with integrity, I will watch over you forever; if you drift away, then there will be no safe place, only a pile of broken stones.' The celebrations are followed by details about further building projects, plus the visit of the Queen of Sheba, who is seriously impressed by what she sees.

If Solomon's life were a Hollywood movie, the closing credits would roll at this point. But it's not. Having got everything a man could need, he continues to look for more – especially wives – and some of these follow different religions.

Once his heart was focused on God, but now his mind and actions wander anywhere. He's warned, but it makes no difference. Enemies emerge, things slide seriously downhill and he dies, a shadow of the man he once was.

Breakdown dead ahead

Solomon's son Rehoboam is the new king and he has the chance to make life easier for the people his father used as forced labour. Instead, he promises to put the boot into the downtrodden even harder.

Bad move. The revolt begins and the country breaks in two – Israel in the north led by King Jeroboam and Judah in the south led by Rehoboam. They're nearly always at war with each other and neither land is a success. Then, the fabulous temple gets attacked and wrecked by the Egyptians, who take everything of value.

Up north, King Jeroboam starts well, but it doesn't last. His arm is paralysed, then healed by a prophet, but the warning is ignored. When his son becomes ill, his wife seeks out another prophet and hears this: 'If your family die in the city, they will be eaten by dogs; if they die in the country, they will be eaten by vultures.' Not the prettiest way to say you'll have no friends left to help you – but clear.

The rulers who follow are a mixed bunch. These include Asa in the south, who has good policies but bad feet, and Baasha in the north, who lives up to the sound of his name by fighting all the time. He's followed by Zimri, who lasts precisely one week before setting fire to both himself and his palace.

Omri follows the fire-starter, and his son becomes King Ahab, who turns out to be the worst of them all. He marries Jezebel, who hates her husband's faith. Ahab may say he respects God, but building a temple to Baal in Samaria looks like a man hedging his bets.

The news-bringer

That's the background for a prophet named Elijah. His first job is to warn King Ahab of drought and then retreat fairly quickly. Being brave will come later. First he lives by a small brook with only ravens for company. When the brook dries up, he receives shelter and help from a widow living with her only son. God miraculously provides their food and, when the boy becomes so ill that he stops breathing, God answers Elijah's prayer with an astonishing healing.

Three years have passed by the time Elijah returns to the capital. King Ahab sees him coming: 'It's the worst troublemaker in this whole drought-ridden land,' he snarls.

'No, your majesty,' responds Elijah. 'Thanks to your wife, you've got Baal instead of God in pride of place here. Get their so-called prophets together and let's see where the power really lies.'

High on Mount Carmel, this is the situation: two stacks of wood, two dead bulls and two sacrifices to God ready to begin. 'It's time to bring fire down from heaven,' says Elijah. 'You lot, first.' Four hundred and fifty prophets of Baal begin dancing and shouting. Result: nothing.

'Perhaps your god's daydreaming… or gone to the toilet,' teases Elijah. 'Try harder.' The yelling continues but there's no answer, no fire.

'Now,' says Elijah, 'come closer.' He starts remaking God's altar that Jezebel had torn down, soaks his offering with buckets of water and calls upon God. The fire from the sky is stunning, burning the wood, the bull, the stones and vaporising every single drop of water. It's the end for the prophets of Baal and the drought. A tiny cloud gives way to a dark sky and the storm of the year.

Mind you, the only vengeance Jezebel wants involves Elijah's head. He flees from her into the desert hills. God looks after him but also gets him to confront his fear.

Elijah faces earthquake, wind and fire… but God doesn't speak through any of them. Instead, there's a small quiet voice asking: 'What are you doing here?' Elijah doesn't get any easy reassurance from God but he does get several jobs, including to work with Elisha, who will be his successor.

Troubles and truth-telling

Ahab's reign continues with success against the Syrian army. Then, there's the small matter of a vineyard belonging to his neighbour, Naboth. Ahab wants it as a vegetable garden; Naboth doesn't want to sell. The king gets depressed so his wife gets busy and, true to Jezebel's track record, Naboth is stoned to death on a trumped-up charge.

Elijah returns with a warning about stealing from your neighbour. Although the king knows this prophet will challenge him, he also knows Elijah tells the truth and, for a while, he mends his ways.

Of course, Ahab takes most of his advice from those who agree with him, but he can't help being fascinated by the awkward truth-tellers sent from God. Micaiah is one of those. He doesn't take the king's request for advice seriously at first but, when he's asked to tell the truth, he warns of death. His reward is a spell in prison, but he's right. The king is hit by a stray arrow and bleeds to death on the battlefield.

The book completes its royal round-up with Jehoshaphat in the south, who was a partial success, and Ahaziah in the north, who proved to be no better than his father, Ahab. So the first book of Kings shows people getting one or two things right but the rest spectacularly wrong. There's also that question from God to his prophet: 'What are you doing here?' It's not just Elijah who has to answer that.

1 Kings – a short guide

People want wealth… preferably with wisdom. King Solomon gets both but it doesn't save him. And those that follow rarely learn the lessons of his life – fine work doesn't make up for bad relationships. Alongside the kings are the prophets, especially Elijah, who calls on God to pour fire from the sky. It works, but it's not how God speaks to his prophet when it matters most. Instead, he chooses a quiet moment and a small voice. Sometimes the noise of life needs to subside for listening to begin.

2 Kings:
down and down

The second part of Kings is, in many ways, darker than the first. The outside threat to the kingdoms comes from the Assyrians and Babylonians. But the leaders of both Israel and Judah seem very capable of wreaking plenty of destruction themselves.

It starts off with a rebellion and King Ahaziah, who falls off a roof garden. From there on in, it gets worse. Does the king pray for healing? No, he tries to consult fake foreign gods about whether he'll get better. The prophet Elijah intercepts his messengers. No need to ask anyone other than God, he tells them. And – if the king wants to know – he isn't going to recover.

After that, the prophet's job passes dramatically to Elisha as a whirlwind sweeps Elijah from everyone's sight and power falls on the new man. The other prophets can't actually believe what they've seen and go looking for their old leader whom God has taken. After three days, they give up and report back that he's really gone. Elisha sighs: 'Didn't I tell you that in the first place?'

His first task is to sort out Jericho's water supply, which is suspected of causing miscarriages and deaths. He purifies the source with salt and the problem is solved.

Skin deep

Much of Elisha's life seems to parallel that of his master Elijah. He's best known for healing Naaman, frontman of the Syrian army who is disfigured by a horrible skin disease. Naaman's work may be brilliant, but he looks revolting.

His wife has a servant girl who was taken from Israel during a raid. Instead of hating everything about the man responsible for her capture, the girl feels sorry for him. 'I know someone who could cure him,' she says. 'He lives where I used to live.'

The result is a big expedition, funded by the king of Syria. Naaman is sent to visit Israel, loaded down with gifts of gold, silver and fabulous clothes, plus a royal letter of introduction. His arrival at the palace terrifies the king of Israel, who thinks he's been sent to create an excuse for more war. 'I'm a monarch, not a doctor,' he wails. Elisha hears about the fuss and sends the king a message: 'Send him to me.'

So Naaman's magnificent travelling party moves on to the prophet's place. Elisha doesn't even come out to greet him. A servant appears with the instruction: 'Wash in the River Jordan – seven times. That should do it.'

Naaman is furious: 'Doesn't he know who I am? He hasn't even come out to see me, much less cure me. And he thinks I'm going to take a dip in that stinking river?'

His servants realise they have to say something. 'Look,' they point out, 'if he'd asked you to do something really difficult, you'd have done it. Right?'

'Absolutely,' says Naaman.

'Then, why can't you do something easy like washing in a river?' So, still mumbling a bit, Naaman begins to do it. After seven doses of the treatment, the change is stunning: clean, healthy skin.

He returns to Elisha to tell him he now knows there really is only one God. Naturally, he wants to give the prophet a big present. Elisha will accept nothing, but tells him that he goes in peace with his blessing.

Elisha's servant, Gehazi, can't believe his boss has passed up such a massive payday. He runs after Naaman, gets money out of him and then lies about it to Elisha. His reward for dishonesty is illness – the same disease that troubled Naaman begins to cover his body.

The killing years

Elisha provides both wise advice and miraculous help for over 50 years. But, in spite of his efforts, these are dark times in a threatened country. Samaria is besieged and its people reduced to eating donkey heads. Even after a miraculous escape, people fail to appreciate the help they've received. Samaria may be God's country, but it's not run by his rules.

Most deaths merely get a mention, but the fall of Queen Jezebel is covered in detail. Her enemies are closing in, so what does the queen do? She puts on eye shadow and fixes her hair. When the assassins arrive, she looks great but it doesn't save her. She's thrown from a window, driven over by chariots and eaten by dogs. By the end, there's nothing identifiable to bury.

Jehu is the man behind the killing, and killing is what he's good at. Jezebel's demise makes it three royals he's eliminated. Next up are 70 descendants of kings, followed by all the prophets of Baal. Their temple is turned into a toilet.

This is a book where the stories of killing seem to mount up endlessly. It's not always the men in charge either. Queen Athaliah plans to kill every single one of her grandchildren and almost succeeds. Threats, even potential ones, are removed at any cost here.

There *are* moments of peace and quiet, such as when King Joash is crowned and the people get their minds set on God alone. It lasts for a while but bad habits always creep back. When Elisha dies, the world isn't much different from how it was when he started.

Warts and all

This is history with the warts on show, where whole families get slaughtered just for being related to the wrong person. King Amaziah is newsworthy because he *doesn't* wipe out hundreds in revenge for the death of his father. 'Parents should not be killed for the crimes of their children,' he declares, 'Children should not die for the crimes of their parents.'

This is basic stuff from Deuteronomy, but somehow it's been lost in the red mist of blood feuds. Kings come and go. Some are better than others, but the worst are truly dreadful. Not even the mothers of unborn babies are safe from slaughter.

The land is in a mess and it's the northern kingdom of Israel that falls first. It's wiped out by the Assyrians, who cart God's people off to slavery and import settlers who will become known as Samaritans, the ones that the Jewish nation will never quite accept because of the differences in their faith.

The attackers turn south to Judah, but King Hezekiah rules there. He takes God seriously and, thanks to the prophet Isaiah, doesn't lose his nerve. The Assyrians get as far as the walls of Jerusalem but no further. Their army, running into hundreds of thousands, is wiped out by an 'angel of death' as it camps outside the gates and the emperor of Assyria withdraws, never to return.

Hezekiah improves life for his people, as he builds a reservoir and a water supply route for Jerusalem. But he makes one fatal mistake: being friendly to visitors from Babylon. Isaiah warns him that the visitors will return with soldiers.

How far we've fallen

Hezekiah is followed by two utterly brutal kings. The third one along, Josiah, sets a far better example. Builders, working on the temple, unearth a book of God's teaching. Josiah is fascinated by it and appalled at how far they've sunk below what's expected. He becomes the great reformer.

The symbol of that change is the return of the great Passover meal, where everyone remembers how their ancestors escaped from slavery in Egypt.

He's less successful as a military commander and the Egyptians defeat him. They become the real power in Judah until the Babylonians sweep in and 10,000 are carried away as slaves.

The last king of Judah is Zedekiah and he begins one final, futile revolt. In response, the temple is burnt down, the palaces wrecked and the city walls broken. Zedekiah has to watch as his sons are killed in front of him. It's the last thing he sees as they stab out his eyes and lead him away, blinded, to prison and exile. With him goes everything of any value.

Things in Babylon ease a little across time, but there is no return to Jerusalem, no happy ending. If you thought, at the start, that it couldn't get any worse, the book is a sobering reminder of just how bad it can become when God gets a back seat in people's lives.

This story isn't the end for God's people… but sometimes it sounds like it. What the book does best is turn the spotlight on two harsh realities:

Rule 1 If God says something, ignore it at your peril.
Rule 2 If you're in a hole, don't keep digging.

2 Kings – a short guide

Do you call on God or your own kind of experts? That's the question at the very start of 2 Kings. And if you do call on God, will you do what he says? This is a world where kings could make a difference but don't, and even the basic laws get lost. In contrast, when Josiah stumbles across those rules, he follows them. Naaman finds God when he loses his ego and Joash discovers the right way when he's doing the right thing. The bright intervals are a sign that life doesn't need to end in tears. The fact that it does is a reminder that happy endings are not automatically guaranteed.

1 Chronicles:
a place to call your own

Chronicles covers some of the ground you meet in the books of Samuel and Kings. But this is a different understanding of the story, with a focus not on who did what and when, but on the good things to be learned from what's happened. It's a bit like a speaker picking out the aspects of a subject that listeners might apply to their own lives.

Pages from the story of God's people. A selection to encourage those returning from exile to Jerusalem: snapshots, prayers, reflections, comments, messages, poems. And lists… really long ones. It's a book to chew over, to take your time with and see what unfolds as the pages turn.

The book starts with a 'who's who' that goes all the way back to Adam. There are occasional notes about who did what and where, but, in essence, this is an enormous family tree. When the stories start, they open up with a king's death.

Saul is hit by arrows from the Philistine army and badly wounded. He doesn't want to become an exhibition piece in an enemy victory parade, so he kills himself, but they find his body and hang his head as a trophy in one of their temples.

The end of Saul is the beginning for David, the most famous of all the kings. He's the man who captures Jerusalem and his best soldiers get a mention. There's special credit for those who can shoot both right- and left-handed: flexibility is a bonus in battles.

The Covenant Chest party

Once he has the land well under control, David wants to bring the Covenant Chest to Jerusalem... but only if it's what God wants. So the beautifully carved chest with the ten great rules goes travelling again: a reminder that God will be with his people if they remain faithful.

As it travels, the people dance along the route, David included. He doesn't always understand God, but, at this stage in his life, he always talks with him. The result is increasing power and success.

When the chest takes the final part of its journey into Jerusalem, there's a song and dance party for God with the best music, the right people and lunch for everyone to round it off. Here's one of the songs.

Be grateful and never forget God's promise:
a home where we can live,
a place to call our own.
We were strangers in a strange land
but he looked after us,
he stayed with us.

One God created the whole of this world,
with earth and sky to spell out his message
and the seas to roar his song.
If trees could talk, they'd shout with joy,
so we put it into words:
God loved us then,
he loves us now,
he'll love us till the end of time.
That's our news and that's our song
for everywhere... for everyone.

Are you sitting comfortably?

Now, it's an odd thought, but when things are going well, someone eventually feels guilty. David tells Nathan, the prophet, that he feels bad because he's got a great place while the Covenant Chest is kept in a tent. An excellent one but, nevertheless, a tent. The prophet, without a moment's thought, replies: 'Well, you're God's man, do something about it.'

Later that evening, God tells the prophet that his place is in a tent because he travels with his people. He hasn't asked for a grand temple and now isn't the time to start building one. That task will fall to the next generation. It's a reminder that you can't hurry God, however well-meaning you may be.

David may have been disappointed, but he's also grateful to God. 'Lord,' he prays, 'I'm not worthy of all you've done for me. There is nobody like you, no story to match our escape from slavery. You're the God of the wonderful promises and that's what gives me the courage to pray to you.'

Victories in battle keep coming but it's not all plain sailing. A census leads to an epidemic and the king seeks forgiveness. The root of the problem isn't clear, but perhaps the census shows David counting on his own strengths and not on God.

You can't do everything

The epidemic prompts the king to buy land in Jerusalem. That's the start of a process which will lead to the building of the temple. David remembers it isn't his job, but he seems desperate to get involved and stacks up tons of construction materials. Then he devises a complex scheme for temple personnel with administrators, musicians, priests and security. It's all fixed up, down to the smallest detail.

As the final chapters unfold, the king draws his team together and tells them how he really wanted to put up a temple for God – in case you hadn't guessed! But too much blood has stained his hands. The building work falls to Solomon.

David's instruction to his people is to go on obeying God so that they can live long in the land. To his son, the message is equally clear: God needs an undivided heart, a willing mind and a determined worker. If you ignore him, it will be over, full stop; but if you seek God, you will always find him.

In spite of all the stuff David's piled up, he remains aware of his limits. He tells God: 'There's nothing any of us can give you that you didn't give us to begin with. You see us as we are and love us best when we're honest and straightforward, through and through.'

The book closes as Solomon takes over, with a nation expectant and a royal back garden piled high with building materials. Not so much an ending, then, as a pause for a deep, deep breath.

The 1 Chronicles takeaway

- You don't have to understand God in order to talk to him.
- God's love doesn't alter: it's the yesterday-today-forever sort.
- You don't have to feel guilty just because you feel comfortable.
- God cares for us even when we feel like strangers in this world.
- You cannot do everything – accept it.

2 Chronicles:
more than buildings

The second part of Chronicles starts and ends with temple-building. In between, it deals with a people who show a very variable faith in God, and kings who offer some seriously flawed leadership. But there is a bright side. People's faith may wobble but God's faithfulness doesn't.

If you've ever worried what your house looks like, you may have some sympathy for Solomon here. He's got to build God's house and getting that work done is a good deal more complicated. There are 80,000 men on quarrying and 70,000 in the transport division – all of that before a stone gets laid.

Solomon thinks big, but he's wise enough to know that even the best building cannot hold God himself. The whole of heaven can't do that, he tells a neighbouring king. It doesn't stop him sourcing gold, silver, bronze and cedar in eye-watering quantities. The roof of the temple seems to reach into the sky itself.

House-warming time

Eventually the building is finished and Solomon can sort out a big event to move the Covenant Chest into its newly finished home. You might have wondered what fabulous mix of valuables this chest holds, but it carries only two stones containing God's top ten directions for living happily and well. Very simple but special, because it's a reminder of God's presence among his people.

Solomon prays to God, who has loved his people, led them to this place and needs their whole-hearted obedience. Even with this stunning temple in all its glory, Solomon finds it hard to imagine God living among them. It doesn't stop him asking that God hears them, helps them and goes on loving them.

After the spectacular festivities, God takes a quiet night-time moment to speak with his king. 'I've heard your prayers,' he tells him, 'and this is my promise. If people are sorry when they do wrong and turn back to me, I will forgive them. And, if you are faithful to me, I will be faithful to you. But, if you all go your own way, your magnificent building will mean nothing at all.'

Later, the Queen of Sheba pays a visit. She's stunned by Solomon's wisdom, bowled over by his food and amazed by the temple.

'I didn't believe what people were saying,' she admits, 'but it's true – it's breathtaking. What a king you are and what a God you have!'

The downhill years

After the boom time with Solomon, the writer of Chronicles moves on to the break-up of the kingdom after his death. It's achieved by Rehoboam, whose tongue runs away from his brain. He's advised to maintain people's loyalty by kindness and consideration. Instead he says he'll horsewhip anyone who doesn't meet his demands. God's people break into two parts: Israel in the north and Judah in the south. No one is ever able to repair that split properly.

In the north, they slip into the worship of other gods and pay for priests who will support this. In the south, things work well for a bit longer but, when everything feels fine, there's a drift away from God.

Some leaders understand the need to stick with God; some don't. King Asa in the south turns to strong neighbours for military backing and to doctors for cures to his illnesses. But he never seems to turn to God. The result is that he finds life hard going.

In contrast, his son, Jehoshaphat, sends out a 16-strong teaching team across Judah to show people exactly what it is that God expects.

Fairness and honesty run through this book. Judges are warned against bribery and taking sides; prophets are told to tell the truth, even when it's unpopular. Prayer also plays an important part, even if it's often only when the people find themselves deep in trouble of their own making.

These are brutal times when leaders seem more likely to be killed by a member of their own family than an enemy. In contrast, when the right men or women are in charge, Jerusalem becomes a quiet place and a safe haven.

The trouble is that it doesn't last. When a good leader dies, people drift off in any old direction and life begins to disintegrate. The prophets sum it up: 'If you aren't with God, then God isn't with you.'

King Amaziah doesn't listen; Uzziah starts steadily but goes downhill and ends up with a dreaded skin disease. Jotham is better but then Ahaz manages to break every rule available to him, from closing down the temple to sacrificing his own children.

Roller-coaster days

When Hezekiah becomes king, he faces a mile-high pile of things to put right but he sets about it with cheerfulness and an eye to detail. The temple is quickly opened for worship again, and the return of the Passover festival, celebrating the nation's escape from slavery, is a total joy.

Not everyone comes back to God's place at once, but the good news about the change soon spreads. Hezekiah is well organised and wants to bring the nation together again. People are amazed by the experience of being looked after so well.

The two kings that follow him are a step backwards, but the third one, Josiah, is better again. He comes across a missing book of the law while repairing the temple and lets the people hear what it says about following God with heart, soul and hands.

The final four kings are a long mudslide into disaster, ending up with the temple burned to the ground and people carried off into slavery. It isn't the last word because the writer finishes with a reminder of how Cyrus, the emperor of Persia, allowed a return to Jerusalem and permitted the rebuilding of the city and its temple.

The story has been a roller-coaster ride. Enthusiasm followed by excess; joy followed by jealousy. The missing ingredient is steadiness: faithfulness from one generation to the next. The book closes with the promise of rebuilding, but you end with a sense of the need for a new way – a spirit and a strength that will carry the work across the years.

The 2 Chronicles takeaway

- Buildings are good, but God is so much better than any place erected to him.
- God's treasure is held in his rules for living well and getting on together.
- Don't let your tongue run away from your brain.
- Seek to be truthful, even if it's unpopular.
- If you want to help people, be sure to be well-organised.

Ezra:
come this far, still so far to go

In terms of what happens when, Ezra seems to follow on from where Chronicles left off. It's not always written in date order, so it can be a bit of a puzzle. What is perfectly clear is that the homecoming of the Jewish people after exile is only the start of the story.

This is the return of God's people to Judah and its great city, Jerusalem. Cyrus, who rules the Persian Empire, opens the action by sending a first group of exiles home: 'May God go with you,' he declares, 'and may he stay with you.'

They're given permission to rebuild the temple and they're backed by hard cash and supplies. Cyrus also uncovers over 5,000 items stolen from the old building. Then the book lists who returns and what they bring with them – 245 mules, 435 camels and 6,720 donkeys. If you like detail, you'll love this writer.

Starting over again

Six months after settling back into their homes, the people come together in Jerusalem for the Festival of Shelters. The temple is still a shell but there's an altar, and they start collecting money for rebuilding.

Soon the foundation stones are laid and trumpets ring out in celebration: soul music of the very earliest variety. They know that God is good and his love goes on forever. The younger ones are full of joy, but the older men and women shed tears. It's been a long road and they remember what's happened along the way.

Those people already in the land are not sure about all this. 'We've been here ever since you were sent into exile,' some of them say. 'We want a part in the rebuilding.'

The offer is refused. 'This is something that we have to do ourselves,' explain the leaders. But opposition begins to grow and the construction work gets halted.

Getting it done

In chapter 4, the book leaps forward to what happens when the temple is finished. It's a complaint from a local governor to the emperor about rebuilding the city walls. He thinks the people are putting up defences before starting a rebellion. Even worse, he's worried that this could lead to them not paying taxes. The work on the walls is stopped.

Jumping back in time, temple construction remains on hold until the arrival of a new emperor, Darius. The world feels like a different place with him in charge and two prophets, Haggai and Zechariah, encourage the builders to start work again. A local governor picks up on this almost at once and demands to know about the planning permission.

It sounds like a major problem, but the governor decides not to stop the project until he's consulted his boss. Darius gets a detailed report including historical background notes and is invited to check it against his own records.

A search turns up the instructions provided by his predecessor, Cyrus, and he sees no reason to interfere. Indeed, he goes further. 'Let them get on with it,' Darius declares, 'and provide the funds needed from the West Euphrates taxation area.'

In case anyone might be sluggish in their support, he commands that anyone who ignores his order should have a beam taken out of their house, sharpened and driven straight through their body. Suddenly, there are very few objections to the work. The building makes good progress and, when it's finished, there's joy all round. They can celebrate their freedom just as Moses did all those years ago.

Done… well, not exactly

Chapter 7 starts with another leap across time. The temple is in place, but hardly any work has been done on the city for two whole generations. It's as if the big building is enough and the city as a whole doesn't matter.

This is where Ezra himself comes into the story. He gets permission from Emperor Artaxerxes for a second group of exiles to return.

Ezra is confident that God will protect them and they get back safely. What they find on their return, however, is not good. Things have come to a complete halt. In part, this is because the leaders have been marrying into other tribes and getting involved in activities that Ezra describes as 'disgusting'. The guilty parties are named and the book ends with a sentence that the scholars can't translate so no one really knows what it means. It's not exactly a very satisfactory finish but this is about life as it happens rather than life in a perfect world.

Two home truths from Ezra

- When you're given a new start, you need to grasp it with both hands.
- Real joy lies in completing the work you were given, not just beginning it.

Nehemiah:
putting it right

Nehemiah is a personal memoir written around the same time as Ezra. They were often kept together on one scroll. But there is a difference. This is not just about building work in Jerusalem; it's also about someone's life.

Question: Who should head up a major rebuilding project in Jerusalem?
Answer: A wine taster in another country.

This is the unlikely story of Nehemiah, a Jew who works in Babylon. He's been promoted to the post of wine taster for Artaxerxes, emperor of Assyria. Nehemiah is the one trusted not to poison the emperor's drinks but also the person who takes a sip to check no one else has done that. So his job involves fabulous free wine and possible sudden death.

It might have stayed that way if it hadn't been for news from back home. Nehemiah hears that Jerusalem, which ought to have been restored decades ago, is still a broken-down wreck of its old self. He's shocked and saddened but not without hope.

'I know we deserved this,' he tells God. 'But you promised that, if we turned back to you, you'd turn back to us. Hear our prayers and may Artaxerxes listen to my request.'

The chance comes when the emperor notices that Nehemiah isn't his usual cheery self. 'What's up?' he asks. 'I've never seen you looking miserable before. Something must have happened.'

After a deep breath and a lightning prayer, Nehemiah tells the boss how his hometown looks more like an ancient ruin than a city.

'So what do you want to do?' asks Artaxerxes.

'If you'd let me,' he replies, 'I'd go and see if I can rebuild it.'

'Agreed,' says the emperor.

Getting back in shape

Nehemiah doesn't make a big thing of his arrival in Jerusalem. But, one night, he gets up with a few friends to take a closer look at the walls. Not a pretty sight, but something people have to face up to.

'We're in trouble,' he tells the leaders, 'and the best place to start is with putting back our city walls.'

Some people think it's madness but, bit by bit, the building work is done. Not flashy, not instant, just steady. Those who were against the plan soon turn nasty: the walls are beginning to look like a proper defence and they feel threatened. Nehemiah has a two-fold response: guards plus prayers.

The builders themselves sing a kind of blues number that tells how tired they are and how much there's always left to do. As those around them keep making threats, Nehemiah arms everyone. They even sleep with their spears.

When it's not enemies muttering about him, it's his own people: 'We've got large families, larger food bills, enormous debts and frightening tax bills.'

It sounds utterly familiar but there's a nasty twist with these problems: 'We're so broke,' people explain, 'that we have to sell our children as slaves just to make ends meet.'

Nehemiah's jaw drops. 'Rich families are allowed to buy people from poor families? That's what enemies do, not friends!'

The leaders look at the ground and say nothing. So the debts that caused the problem are cancelled – everyone will start again. It's typical of his leadership. Profit doesn't matter most; making
sure people are fed and cared for does.

Summer festival time

Eventually, everything is sorted. The walls are complete and the city gates are back in place.
The people gather for their harvest celebrations, the Feast of Shelters, and to listen to what God
requires of them.

This includes not just the words themselves but a straightforward explanation of what they actually
mean. Hearing the message expressed so simply moves and saddens them as they realise how far
they have to go. But it's not a time for grief: the people are encouraged to eat, drink, share what
they have with others and just enjoy themselves.

The people also realise how they used to camp under the stars to celebrate harvest. It sounds
like a good idea so they try it… and the place buzzes with excitement, joy and fresh air! It doesn't
mean that all problems are swept away. It takes time for them to admit they're part of what's gone
wrong. A poem that's also a prayer captures the heart of it:

> *You alone made the stars and sky, the sea and earth,*
> *you chose and changed us, worked the miracles we needed,*
> *you gave us our direction, kept the promises you made.*
>
> *Yet our families forgot you, went their own way.*
> *Slavery in Egypt seemed better than freedom with you.*
> *Still you did not abandon them*
> *but let them prosper and succeed*
> *and still they disobeyed.*
> *That's why you let them be conquered.*

Even then you did not forsake or destroy them.
Your mercy is great, your love without end.
But it is right that we have been punished:
We did not listen, we have sinned.

What next?

The confession is followed by a commitment to change. This includes:

- an end to trading that leaves no time for rest
- arrangements to stop debt piling up forever
- fair resourcing for temple activities.

These are simple steps to ensure that God is not neglected in his rebuilt city.

Not everyone can fit inside the city walls, so Nehemiah sets out to ensure that everyone has a place somewhere. When he eventually returns to wine-drinking duties with the emperor, everything is in good shape.

A return visit later on is not so encouraging. He catches one priest letting out a room in the temple to his friend, while some temple musicians are without regular work as there's not enough money to pay them. In addition, the sabbath day is beginning to look like just another chance to go shopping.

Even worse, because of intermarriage, their whole way of life is breaking down and their language itself is at risk. It's as if the old cycle of trying hard and slipping back has begun all over again. Nehemiah does what he can to put things back on a proper footing, then asks God not to forget what he has done.

And that's the end of the book. You could say it's about getting a city back in shape, but it's also about giving people back the confidence to seek God: building faith as well as walls.

Nehemiah in a nutshell

Nehemiah: a wine taster who cared deeply about his homeland and turned prayer into action. He was also a person who worked out where to start and then kept going. This is a book that highlights justice but doesn't ignore poetry. It's a story that recognises how easy it is to slip back into old routines but speaks with passion about better ways of life.

Esther:
special delivery

What happened yesterday is not always what happens today. When the earlier parts of the Old Testament were written, having more than one wife was not uncommon. It often didn't work very well, as David and Solomon found out. By the time of Jesus, the pattern had become one man – one woman. However, this is Esther – different and frankly a one-off.

The setting is the winter palace of King Xerxes, the very wealthy ruler of Persia and 127 other places. Xerxes decides to organise two enormous parties: one for the gentlemen, that he hosts, and another for the ladies, hosted by his favourite wife, Queen Vashti.

Towards the end of the feasting, the king calls the queen across. He wants his friends to see how fabulous she is. For whatever reason, Vashti refuses to come. Big mistake. It becomes an issue about respect and, to be honest, about male egos. Either way, it's the end of the queen's time as number-one wife.

Love quest

The start of the search for a replacement is a bit like a reality TV series with a full year of makeovers. One of the contestants is Esther, a Jewish girl raised by her cousin Mordecai since her parents died. It's not easy being Jewish in Persia, so Mordecai advises her not to mention it.

When the time comes for the finalists to meet the king, they are sent to him one by one. Esther is not the only beautiful girl, but there's something special about her. She's the one who wins both the king's affection and the position of queen.

By this time, Mordecai is working in the palace and overhears people plotting to murder the king. He warns Esther, who tells her husband, the king. The result is the execution of the two would-be killers.

The killing plot

Some while later, Haman becomes prime minister and everyone is expected to bow down at the Royal Gate in his honour. The only one who doesn't is Mordecai. 'Why don't you kneel?' he demands.

'I'm Jewish,' he tells him. No other explanation is needed. This is the tribe that will worship just one God… and no one else.

Haman is not the best person to cross. 'We need a way,' he tells his team, 'to remove every single Jew.' The plan starts with a complaint to the king that there are people who don't join in and just break the law when they feel like it. Haman suggests that getting them out of the way could make the country a better place and save money.

'Get on with it,' says the king, 'and you can keep the cash.' It looks like Haman has got himself a result, twice over.

A circular is issued, under the king's seal, with the details of the slaughter. While people are reeling from the news, the king and his prime minister are enjoying a quiet drink within the palace walls.

When Mordecai hears the news, he contacts Esther and begs her to appeal to the king. Now, that's easier said than done. Going to visit Xerxes without being invited means death unless he happens to be in a good mood and waves you in. Even for one of the king's favourites, it's a terrible risk.

Esther tells Mordecai that it's a full month since Xerxes has asked for her. In return, he tells her bluntly that doing nothing isn't an option. Maybe, he suggests, you were made queen for a moment like this. So, after fasting and prayer, Esther takes a deep breath, puts on her best dress and walks in to see the king.

Wine and hanging time

Esther catches him in a good mood. In fact, he's so pleased to see her that he offers her anything she wants, up to half his empire. All she asks for is that he and Haman be her guests at a special banquet. The wine flows that evening and the king repeats his offer of a big present. She only asks that the two of them eat with her the next night, too.

On the way back from the first banquet, Haman is full of himself, so he's infuriated to come across Mordecai, who still doesn't bow to him. His wife suggests that he gets a really big gallows built. 'And when that's done,' she says sweetly, 'ask the king to let you hang Mordecai from the very top of it. That should cheer you up!'

Meanwhile, the king is unable to sleep, so he calls for someone to read from his family history book. The section he hears includes a bit about how Mordecai saved the king from being killed.

'What did we do for him?' he asks.

'Umm… nothing, your majesty' is the answer.

'Are any of my officials around?' he barks.

Now Haman has just returned to the palace to get permission for the hanging. Bad timing.

'There's someone I want to honour,' says the king. Haman is delighted because he thinks the king is talking about him. 'I want the person dressed in the best clothes and brought to me in the grandest style possible.'

At the moment when Haman's chest is so puffed up that he's almost ready to burst, the king mentions Mordecai. Haman can hardly believe it, but he has no choice other than to follow orders. Mordecai gets a long chat with the king that is only ended when it's time for the second banquet.

Surprise party

Once again, the king has a good evening and offers his queen whatever she wants. 'I don't like troubling you,' she confesses, 'but there is one thing. It's just that I want to go on living… and so do my people. We've been sold, not for slavery, but for slaughter. It's almost time for our extermination.'

'Who dares to do something like this?' he roars.

'The answer is right here,' she tells him. 'It's Haman.'

The king is so furious he storms out into the garden to cool off. While he's out there, Haman throws himself on Esther, begging for mercy. Returning from the garden, the king gets the wrong impression. 'Do you think you're going to molest the queen right in front of me?' he yells.

The guards cover Haman's head and one of them points out the gallows that Haman has built to hang Mordecai.

'Then you know what to use it for,' hisses the king. Once Haman is hanging high in the air, the king calms down a bit.

The royal seal

At last, Esther has a chance to tell the king about her background and her family. Now that Haman is gone, the outlook ought to be good, but it's not that simple. An order to kill the Jewish people is still in place. A royal decree cannot be revoked, even by the king. But that doesn't stop him giving people the right to fight back if attacked.

'Say what you wish in my name,' says Xerxes to his queen.

The message goes out immediately and the Jewish people are suddenly no longer a downtrodden minority. The result is that, where it comes to any fights, the Jews come out on top. Now, although the royal seal of approval has included permission to take whatever they want from their enemies, the people take nothing. All they want is the deep joy of being delivered from a death sentence.

And that's what they get. The book finishes with Mordecai as a popular prime minister and the sheer pleasure for Esther and her people of feeling safe and secure at last.

Unravelling Esther

A beauty contest, a murder plot, impending mass slaughter, private dinners, wrong impressions and an unexpected execution – the elements of Esther sound like the plotline for a high-octane TV drama. But within all its twists and turns, there is one thing in Esther's life that nearly everyone has to face: the need to be honest and speak up about who we truly are. For Esther, that means putting her life on the line for her family and her people.

Job:
nightmare days

This is the beginning of the five wisdom books in the Bible, which cover suffering, love, boredom, hate, delight, prayer, parenting and sex – among other things! They do not set out to solve everything but are places where people's puzzles, pain and pleasure are given a voice. Job comes first, struggling with the big issues of suffering and fairness.

Job: a decent man with a great family, a nice place and plenty of money. It's easy to believe in God when life's like that, but what if it wasn't so comfortable? That's the real challenge. When Job loses his children and his wealth in the course of a single day, it's sickening and terrifying, but he doesn't blame God.

Then he breaks out in sores all over his body, the sort that drive you mad if you don't rub them and get far worse if you do. Why on earth is God allowing this to happen? His wife scorns his trust in the almighty. Job doesn't agree. He knows how we welcome all the good things when they come, so why should we complain when there's times of troubles?

Not deserved

Three friends come to visit. They intend to cheer him up, but he looks so awful they're lost for words and just sit with him. At last, Job breaks down. Everything he's dreaded is coming true and he curses the day he was born. In response, his friends seem stuck for something helpful to say. All they manage is pious advice and criticism.

Eliphaz assumes that it's all Job's fault: 'People bring problems on themselves as surely as sparks fly in a fire.'

'I just don't deserve this,' Job replies. 'I've been conscripted into an army of endless suffering. When I lie down, I can't sleep. If I do, I'm drowned in nightmares.'

Bildad waits a moment and asks: 'Have you got it off your chest? If *you* haven't done something wrong, it must be your children. If you *are* good, as you claim, everything will work out in time. Our life is like a brief shadow, but God will never make evil strong or abandon the faithful.'

'Yes, yes,' replies an exasperated Job. 'But how can a person make a case against God? He can't! I'm innocent but it looks as if I'm guilty. Frankly, I'm sick of living. Do you know what I think? When an innocent person dies, God laughs. I honestly wish I'd never been born.'

Zophar cuts in: 'An avalanche of words doesn't make you right. You're almost certainly being punished less than you deserve. Get your heart right. Turn away from evil. Reach out to God.'

'That's about as useful as having a doctor who can't heal anyone,' observes Job. 'I may end up dead but God is still my hope – so here's my challenge to him. Why do you hide your face from me? How many wrongs have I committed? Why have I become your enemy? We're set adrift in this world with too few days and too many troubles. How can life begin again when all you can see is death? Trees may manage it, but is it possible with people? You seem to wear everything down, Lord… including us.'

Take pity

The second round of the discussion gets no further than the first. Eliphaz calls Job an old windbag. 'Plus', he says, 'you're not as pure as you claim. Nobody is. Being troublesome breeds trouble.'

'If you and I swapped places,' snaps Job, 'I could nod wisely and say the same things, but it wouldn't help. It only makes the pain worse. Lord, you've left me looking like a skeleton. No wonder people think I'm guilty.'

'Can't you ever be quiet?' Bildad asks. 'God's not going to change to please you. Wicked people get it in the neck. That's what happens. Get used to it.'

'You're supposed to help,' replies Job. 'Instead, you think you're better than me. It's bad enough that God has left me in this hole and that I disgust my family, but you're my friends. Take pity on me. And trust me – one day I *will* meet God.'

Zophar is not impressed. In his eyes, miserable men are bad men. He can't get beyond the idea that you get what you deserve.

'Listen,' Job tells him, 'You *know* some wicked people grow old in comfort. Things aren't always fair in this world.'

Think what I did

The next part of the book shows how, once you've got a good discussion going, it doesn't always lead anywhere. Job is treated as a first-rate failure and a greedy maggot of a man.

'How helpful you've been to someone who's weak and weary!' he observes with deep sarcasm. 'Such vast understanding!'

Job is equally angry with God, who doesn't seem ready to sort anything out. He rounds off by reminding his friends of what he used to do.

'I listened, I helped, I was fair. If people were in rags, I put coats on their backs; if people were down, I encouraged them. I haven't even thought terrible things, much less done them.'

Job's friends see that they're not going to change his mind. As they shrug their shoulders, a younger man, called Elihu, steps forward to point out that they have not answered the challenge. Repeating standard opinions is not a way of answering heartfelt cries.

He summarises what Job has said but tells him how much greater God is than any of us, taking water from the earth and shaping it into clouds, hurling lightning across the sky and letting thunder echo behind it.

The cloud counter

As if on cue, God's voice is heard from the heart of a storm. 'Stand up, Job,' he commands. 'Were you there when I made the world? In the dawn of time when the stars sang together, who put everything in place? Can you count the clouds? Do you give creatures their strength or speed?'

The questions continue and, when it's over, it is Job's turn. All of a sudden, he doesn't want to speak. 'Lord,' he replies, 'I've said too much already.'

So God returns to his questioning. 'Are you trying to prove that I am wrong and you are right? Can you control the wild things or sort out the wicked? '

'No, Lord,' he answers, 'the strength is yours. Now I've seen you, I'm ashamed of how I've gone on and on. I'm sorry.'

The twist

The twist is that God isn't angry with Job. It's the friends who have been full of religious words and short of any helpfulness who infuriate the Lord. Nevertheless, they are forgiven and Job is restored to prosperity. In fact the last part of his life is better than the first.

At the end, he is still challenging the conventional thinking of his day as he makes sure his daughters inherit as well as his sons.

Did Job get explanations about what had happened to him? Not really. But he saw God. And, at that moment, he knew that sometimes you need to trust, even at times when nothing makes sense.

Unlocking Job

Job – the place where the questions get asked about why life seems so unfair and why good people suffer. It's also the book which discovers that there are no neat answers to that. What you do learn is how shallow some of the arguments about suffering can be. If people are in pain, they simply don't want religious platitudes or an enthusiasm for apportioning blame. They need someone who will stick by them.

Psalms:
soul music

Five poetry collections from across nearly 500 years. From private emotions to public statements, you'll find almost every conceivable feeling about God in these 150 psalms. Explanations vary about where and when they were originally sung or said, but what unites them is that they're from life and for life.

What is it that God's looking for? Someone who isn't ducking and diving, someone who doesn't blame everyone and everything else, who keeps their promises even when it costs a lot. That's just one of the voices from Psalms, a collection which starts by admiring how steady people are a blessing as they grow in understanding, and finishes off with everything and everyone celebrating what God has done. Here's just some extracts from those voices to get you started.

Songs of joy (from Psalm 33)

Don't do what you've always done;
sing a new song to God and make it loud with joy
for the Lord who made the sun, moon and stars.
He is the one whose work is built to last,
who loves what's good and fair and trustworthy,
who protects us with unceasing love.

Save me (from Psalm 25)

Keep your promise, Lord: forgive me,
not just for one sin but for many.
Turn to me and be merciful.
Lift the worries that hollow out my heart
and save me from my troubles.
Look at the state I've got myself into
and forgive me
so that today I may walk the path you choose for me.

Glorious (from Psalm 115)

Our God goes wherever he wishes;
his faithfulness enables us;
his constant love protects us.
Others make gods of silver and gold,
then place them proudly in their home.
Their gods have mouths that do not speak,
ears that do not hear, feet that cannot walk.
They are a mirror to the lives
of those who have designed them.
Our God is the one not made by human hands
and he is glorious.

My home (from Psalm 23)

Still waters, good places and time to catch my breath:
you feed me and revive me, Lord.
Like a shepherd cares for his sheep, you hold me close.

Guide me where I should be and keep me safe from evil.
Even in the shadows of death, you are there.
Your love always holds a welcome for me
and your home is my home
forever.

The weight of sorrows (from Psalm 13)

How much longer must I wait, Lord?
Are you always going to forget me?
Is there no end
to the weight of sorrows that break my heart?
Those who hate me smile at the state I'm in:
someone with nothing left to live for.
Look at me, Lord! Answer me.
Give me back the strength I once had.
Then I can be glad again,
I can sing to you of rescue
and the love that never lets me go.

Lost and found (from Psalm 107)

Wherever you are lost, God will bring you back.
In a desert without any tracks, he will find a way for you.
However long you've drowned in darkness,
he will lift you out of your distress.
No matter how strong the door you're trapped behind,
God will break right through.

Clean again (from Psalm 51)

Have mercy on me, Lord.
In the light of your unfailing love,
wipe away what I've done wrong.
I know all too well what that is – I can't forget it
and I deserve to be punished.
Wash me clean again,
create pure thoughts in me once more.
Don't send me away; help me to speak for you again.
How can I repay you for all this?
Only with my deep sorrow for how I've hurt you.

Here I am (from Psalm 40)

I waited patiently; you heard me.
I was sinking into quicksand; you hauled me out
and put me back on solid ground.
There is no one else at all like that.
Yet you don't require a great show of religion,
you want me to listen;
you don't require expensive gifts,
you want me to say: 'Here I am.'

The breath of love (from Psalm 103)

God blesses me with mercy;
his love keeps me alive;
his breath makes me feel young enough
to rise on wings like eagles fly.

He does not punish us as we deserve
or go on and on as he puts us right.
He is slow to anger
and his love will never falter.

Dance again (from Psalm 30)

I was as low as it gets… you lifted me.
I was wounded… you healed me.
I was staring over the edge… you held on to me.
That's why I sing, that's why I feel secure:
because I called and you answered,
because you took my tears and made me dance again.

My safe keeper (from Psalm 121)

I lift up my eyes to the hills.
Is that where my help comes from?
My help comes from the Lord, who made heaven and earth.
He will not let you lose your footing;
he who protects you will not stop watching over you.
Believe me: the Lord who keeps everyone safe
will never be found sleeping when you need him.
He is your shade in the heat of the midday sun
and your light in the darkness of the night.
The Lord will guard you from every danger, every evil
and will preserve your soul.
He will be there when you set out
and still be waiting when you return,
not just today but forever.

Psalms at heart

Wherever you're lost,
whatever has happened,
whenever you're troubled,
his love will not falter.

However you feel,
however you've failed,
whenever you call,
God will be there.

Proverbs:
electricity for the brain

This is a book of wise one-liners: sayings to make you stop and think. It's actually a collection of collections from across centuries. That explains why a lot of things get repeated in a slightly different form. It's a bit like a swimming pool – somewhere to take a regular dip.

Five questions

What is far worse than being a complete idiot?
Being a complete idiot and not realising it.

Who's got bruises, bloodshot eyes and a string of whinges?
Mr 'Just one more drink': that's who.

How can you deal with someone else's anger?
Gentle words outclass a 'don't care' attitude every time.

Why don't some people get along with others?
Because they're only interested in themselves.

And what is more valuable than silver and gold?
Knowing what you're talking about.

Keep your mouth in shape

The trouble with gossip is that it's so tasty
And we don't just nibble it, we swallow it whole.

Give up on double talk;
Dump the dishonesty and look people straight in the eye.

Cruel words crush the spirit; kind words bring you back to life.

The more you talk, the more likely you are to say something you shouldn't.
Open your mouth and you'll have to accept the consequences – good or bad.

Arguments are like cracks in the walls of dams: sort it out before it goes any further.

Lies have only a short life; truth has no 'use by' date, no 'best before' limit.

Uncomfortable words

You won't succeed by covering things over when you do wrong.
Admit it's happened, because that's what makes God's mercy possible.

Some days we need the pain, if we're ever to make the change.

When disasters strike people you dislike, don't smile and say, 'I told you so.'
That's gloating: something God has no time for.

Bright people like to know when others think they are wrong;
It's only stupid people who don't listen.

If you don't hear the poor when they cry out, how on earth do you think you will be heard?

We have a mind *plus* a conscience. It's to stop us hiding from ourselves.

Some people ruin their lives by what they do, then promptly blame God for their own stupidity.

Work rate

Asking a lazy person to do something is about as enjoyable as getting smoke in your eyes.

There's always a risk in life but if you keep using that as a reason for not doing anything, you're not careful, you are lazy.

In the summer, watch the ants. Nobody tells them what to do, but they store food because they know the winter will come. Prepare yourself. Don't just twiddle your thumbs or snooze your life away.

It's better to do an ordinary job and make a living than to act as if you're great and get no work.

Lazy people want things but don't get them. Good stuff comes to those who put in a good shift.

This way or that

Being broke for the right reasons beats being rich for the wrong ones, and a vegetable stew with people you love is better than a five-star banquet with those you don't.

Friends mean well even when they upset you.
If enemies start being pleasant, watch out!

Stupid people talk nonsense; bright people make learning attractive.

Get the wrong person to pass on a message and you've got heartache.
Choose the right one and you'll find peace.

Hate likes to stir up more and more unrest;
Love lets go of the wrong that's done to it and looks to the future instead.

Muscle and cash

Give me just enough: too much and I may start to act as if I own the place, too little and I may take what isn't mine.

Get rich quick, lose it quicker; earn it the hard way and money sticks with you.

Bosses who grind down the poor are like driving rain flattening the crops.

Aggressive people may get rich quick but they end up hurting themselves.
Those who help others get helped when they need it.
Give to the poor and you'll find you still have enough.

The big ifs

If you avoid punishing your children, you're not showing the love you should.
If you want them to finish up right, get them started out right in the first place.

If you know about something and don't say anything, you become part of the problem.
If you are open about troubles when they happen, you'll unblock the road to peace.

If you don't have the right tools, you won't get the right result.

If you understand this world, you'll want to know more. If you don't understand it, you'll be happy to hear the chatter of a thousand opinions that have no foundation in fact or common sense.

Uncommon sense

Sensible people think before forming a view; stupid people believe anything.

Everyone says they're a real friend; try to find one who actually is.

Being cheerful keeps you fit; being gloomy dries up your life.

The right word at the right time is simply a joy.

Telling someone to cheer up when they're really depressed is about as sensible as getting them to take their clothes off when it's nine below zero.

Foolishness wants to have a go at everything.
Wisdom focuses on the one thing that needs to be done.

Enthusiasm without knowledge is impatience – deep waters ahead!

If you want to be close to God, listen to what he's got to say, do what he would do.
Love as he does and you'll know how much he loves you.

The don't list

Don't tell someone you'll help them tomorrow if you can help them today.

Don't write other people off. If you feel negative, keep it to yourself.

Don't grind yourself into the ground trying to make money.
It disappears a lot faster than you can hold on to it.

Don't always make a big thing about tomorrow. Just enjoy the surprises that each day brings.

And don't bank on what you think *you* know. Stick with what God shows you.

Never stop

A good idea, clearly explained, sparkles just as much as the best jewellery.

The difference between people is not whether they sometimes do bad things.
The difference is whether they care about it and want to be forgiven.

Keep your mind open: when you stop learning, you'll forget even what you already know.

Your joy is all yours, your bitterness too; no one owns them or affects them… except you.

Proverbs: three favourites

- Speak up for people who cannot do that for themselves; stand up for the ones who are helpless. They need the protection of people like you.

- Write faithfulness on the pages of your heart; bind loyalty into the very core of who you are.

- When you're doing the right thing, you are like sunlight at dawn: making things lighter and then a bit brighter still.

Ecclesiastes:
life before death

It's quite a long way into the story of the Bible before the thought emerges that there might be life after death. So Ecclesiastes is trying to answer the question of what we make of life here, if it's all we have. The writer sometimes gets labelled as grumpy, but there's a lot more here than a sigh and the shake of a head.

How on earth do you make sense of this world? What do you get at the end of the day for all the work that you do? A short journey on the roundabout of the world – the place where the sun keeps on turning, the wind keeps blowing and nothing ever seems to get finished.

That's how the collection of thoughts called Ecclesiastes kicks off. Nothing is unrealistically rosy here. If you haven't got enough when you count your money the first time, you still won't have enough when you count it again. And, if you're the person who seems to know everything, you'll also understand how much nonsense there is in this world.

Pleasure does you no good, drinking doesn't cheer you up and even amazing projects aren't amazing once you've finished them. Look at me, says the writer. I got what I wanted; I was proud of what I achieved. In the end, it meant no more than chasing the wind.

Turn, turn, turn

It's better to be sensible than stupid but, at the end of it all, everyone's together in the same cemetery. However rich you become, it's your children who will spend it all… and you can't choose them.

Work and worry are what drive our lives. Small wonder we can't sleep at night. So remember it is God who has set this world spinning.

> *There is a time for birth, a time for death;*
> *a time for fighting, a time for healing;*
> *a time for breaking down and a time for building up;*
> *one day for sorrow and another for joy;*
> *one for grief and another for dancing;*
> *one for making love and one for waiting.*
> *God sets the time for everything we do,*
> *for every purpose under heaven.*

Of course, we'd like to know what the future holds but we don't. All we can do is be happy and make the best of what we've got. Eat, drink and enjoy what you've worked for. It is God's gift to you.

It's not fair

Injustice can sometimes make the world seem like an ocean of tears. But look around you: being alone is miserable. Being together, you strengthen each other, you warm each other, you help each other to cope.

Don't be surprised when government officials look after their own little world rather than the people who really need them. Don't go chasing money – all it will do is keep you awake at night. Instead, keep your promises – that's what pleases God. And be satisfied with what is yours or you'll always be straining after what you haven't got. Being good is better than just smelling good; criticism from those who are intelligent is better than praise from those who are daft; something you've actually finished is better than something you've only just begun.

You can tell your brain is going rusty when you moan that things were so much better back in the good old days. Life's a mixture. When things go well, be glad; when troubles come, learn from them. Nobody gets it right all the time, but you can be sure of this: God creates us to be plain and straightforward, while we delight in making things tricky and complicated.

Anything can happen to anyone, so it's no good going on about things not being fair. Remember you're *here*, not six feet under, so celebrate life with the ones you love, every unpredictable day of it. The fastest don't always win the race, the bravest don't always win the battle, the brightest don't always become the boss. But fortune changes: you could be tomorrow's big news.

Time please

Don't create problems by what you do: they'll simply come back to haunt you. Accept how things are and don't wait for exactly the right time to act. It doesn't exist. Get on with work whenever you can and be grateful for every year you live.

Learn to treasure the God who created you while you're still young enough to enjoy what he's created. Don't wait for the dismal days when you don't enjoy life, when your body trembles, your legs fail and your teeth fall out. By then, you'll not hear a thing properly during the day, no matter how loud it is. Then, if you ever do sleep at night, a single bird-call will be enough to disturb you.

We return to where we came from. At the end, you'll know that life is like a short breath. So the wisdom we gather should help us to hold our life together and prod us in the right direction. But don't just go on reading everything – you'll become informed but exhausted. Hold on to the heart of the matter. You were created to give God his place in your life. All you have to do is let it happen.

Ecclesiastes at heart

This world goes round and round, so it's no good trying to stop it. Make the most of what you have. Life may not be all you might want it to be, but it's what you've got. Use it; cherish it; enjoy it with the ones you love. That's God's gift to you.

Song of Songs:
the word is love

Love poetry in the Bible? Absolutely – right here. Some see parallels with the strength of God's love for us. But, firstly, Song of Songs is a book about how love thunders past our uncertainties and fears. It's thought that the poetry was used at marriage celebrations which could last a week, so there'd have been plenty of time for something like this.

'I love you, but I don't deserve you; I'm not good enough' – that's how she explains her feelings.

'You're more amazing than you'll ever imagine and I love you to bits' – that's his reply.

'Place your lips upon my lips,' she asks:

'Touch me, kiss me.
Let me taste how sweet you are,
let me breathe in the scent of your body.
Then take me away and lie me upon your bed.'

Not good enough

Her passion, however, is not matched by her confidence:

'I know I am not pale and elegant like the young women of the city,
but I long for you to tell me I am beautiful too.'

Only the wealthy could afford to be pale. The rest had to work in the fields where the sun weathered their skin. She isn't rich, so she knows she doesn't look like those in the pages of a fashion magazine. But everyone measures beauty differently, and the man she desires feels passionately that she is gorgeous:

> 'My love, you are lovely,
> the way you walk is enough to turn heads,
> the curls in your hair are as fine as golden rings,
> your eyes have the softness of a dove.'

She isn't convinced:

> 'I am not one of those picture-perfect ladies;
> I'm like one of the poor wild roses that struggle to grow
> in the scrubland where our sheep graze.'

The hard work of helping her family to scrape a living means it's tough for her to believe that she's beautiful. Yet, he calls her a rose among thorns because he's seen how her eyes shine with love and his heart is thrilled.

Not all sunshine and flowers

Not everything here sounds romantic by today's standards. You may not want your cheeks compared to pomegranates, your teeth to a flock of sheep or your nose to a tower. But people see beauty in different ways. The poems are not all sunshine and flowers, either. There are the times she longs to be held but he isn't there. Then her fears multiply:

> 'I dreamt of him at night but I couldn't find him.
> I went wandering through the city,
> searching the shadows in every corner.
> I asked and asked those keeping watch:

has he been here? Have you seen him?
Then, as I turned, I saw him, held him tight
and swore I wouldn't let him go.'

It's not just a matter of finding each other. There is a time for love and a time to pause. But waiting is an agony when you are weak with passion.

'Never awaken love,' she declares, 'until the time is right and you are ready.' Yet the whole book is drenched in the longing to love without a moment's delay. Others may have great riches or power, but all the lovers need is each other.

Keynotes in Song of Songs

Love can't be bought, it can't be sold,
it can't be drowned by oceans and floods.
It cannot even be broken by death.
If there is one thing that will win through,
it is love.

Isaiah:
the light and the dark

The books known as the prophets start with Isaiah. Prophecy is not only about the future but also about telling how it is today. This writer comes from Judah, the southern kingdom, where a major change of heart seems to be seriously overdue. Isaiah includes poetry, prayer, history, political comment, visions and calls to repentance, but very little chronological order. Yet the best moments here are as good as it gets.

The prophet Isaiah begins with the hard truth about what has happened in his world. People have filled up their lives with money and selfishness, yet they're loaded down with guilt. What puzzles him is why they do it. They don't feel good, they don't look good and their country is in a mess.

There seems to be a feeling that doing religious activities for a few hours will solve their problems. Don't concentrate on getting your religion right, says Isaiah. Concentrate on getting your life right. Give prayer a break until you've cared for those who need your help.

The end of the party

The message from God is that he can make things right again, but only if they let him. Peace is not about peace and quiet; it's about justice, fairness and getting disputes settled. A better future needs people focused on God, not on the latest fashion.

'What's it to be?' asks God. 'Stuff you've found yourself or the good things I long to give you?'

It looks like an easy choice, but these people opt for a good time rather than the goodness of their God. However, the party is almost over and one day soon people will be glad simply to own the clothes on their backs.

The messenger

Isaiah sees a vision of the Lord surrounded by six winged creatures. He's terrified and thinks it's the end. But one of the creatures touches his lips with fire and tells him: 'Your guilt is gone, your sins are forgiven.'

When the Lord then asks, 'Who shall I send? Who will be my messenger?'

Isaiah replies, 'I will go. Send me.'

He probably regretted it the moment he got the first message, which was for the king. It said: no matter how much you listen, you're not going to understand; no matter how much you look, you'll not get what's happening.

Isaiah wants to know from God how long it's going to be like this. Until the cities are ruined, he's told, until the land is almost empty. But there is some hope. When a tree is cut down, a stump remains and growth can start again. Even in the worst moments, there's the promise of a new beginning.

The king is panicked by the warnings he's received but makes no changes. So Isaiah tells him to remember this: a young woman will have a child, will call him 'God with us' and, by the time he's a young man, he'll have fallen on hard times in a place overgrown with thorn bushes, a country where sheep no longer graze.

Justice first

These are troubled days, but Isaiah is told not to be afraid. People will drift. They will trust in anything but God; they'll blame anyone but themselves. But it will not always be like that. One day, the people who walk in darkness will see a great light; dawn will break for those who live in a land as dark as death. The sign will be a child, one who will be called Wonderful Guide, Mighty God, Everlasting Father, Prince of Peace.

Sadly, the good news is about the future. The current headlines are about punishment burning like a fire through the land. It's not a surprise. If you show no pity for those who need help, if your laws make the rich richer and the poor poorer, what can you expect?

A land of justice is required where the king doesn't judge by appearances or listen to rumours. In this new world, the wolf will lie down with the lamb and everyone will live together in safety and in peace.

The prophecies are not just for God's people. Ten other nations are warned about famine, war, drought and plague. Babylon is told this: hyenas will howl in your palaces, worms will be your blanket and maggots your bed. The proud and the strong everywhere will melt into nothing if they ignore God.

Better days

Amid all the tough talking, there are glimpses of a better time with people firm in their faith and safe in the knowledge that God is their rock. Future hope, though, doesn't improve today's behaviour.

God's people seem to be far more afraid of their enemies than of God himself. So the prophet prays for mercy. If there's any hope, any protection, any safety in times of trouble, it will come from God. And, now and then, amidst the warnings and the darkness, poetry breaks out:

There will come a day,
when the desert will sing for joy
and flowers will bloom in the wild places,
those that are weary will be tired no more,
those that are discouraged will find God's rescue.
The blind will see,
the deaf will hear,
those who cannot walk will run and jump and dance,
those who cannot speak will sing and shout for joy.
The dry plains will be filled with streams of water
and there will be a different kind of road.
Not a street for the foolish who have no time for God
but a way back to a world without sorrow for all who love him.

The politics don't look as good as the poetry. Assyrians are now threatening King Hezekiah. A combination of prayer and help from God sorts it out, but then Hezekiah tries to get friendly with the Babylonians. Bad choice. Having lost an old enemy, he creates a new one without realising it.

Exiles

The second part of the book offers comfort for a people who are now in exile. Babylon has turned on Israel and sucked the best people into its cities. They are the slaves who do all the dirty jobs that no one else wants to do. Although things have gone horribly wrong, there *is* a route back. A voice is crying out in the wilderness to prepare a way. People may wither and die like wildflowers, but God's words will never fade away.

The Lord will take care of his people like a shepherd, gently carrying them in his arms. He is more than we can measure, more than we can understand. This is the one who never grows weary. In his strength, we will rise on wings like eagles, we will run and not grow weary, we will walk and not grow weak.

Isaiah's message also reminds his lost people that they are not forgotten and that someone will come – not a fighter but a servant. He won't need to shout in the streets because people from near and far will want to hear his teaching. The prisoners will be set free, the blind will see and a light will burn in every nation. When people have stolen all you once had, it's not easy to believe such things. But the promise of salvation has not disappeared.

'Don't be afraid,' says the Lord, 'I will save you. I have called you by name and you are mine.'

The promise doesn't sweep away the problems and God knows how easily people fall back on nostalgia. Don't cling to what happened in the past, he tells them. Look for the new thing that I am going to do. The prophet sees a messenger striding across the mountains bringing the good news that people are returning to Jerusalem. Even the broken stones of the ruined city will be shouting for joy.

Change of heart

Alongside this glimpse of triumph, there is another image. It is a single servant, without dignity, without beauty, like a plant trying to survive in dry ground. This is someone who is despised and rejected.

It's not his fault. People say that it should have been us. We were in the wrong, not him, and yet he took our punishment. He took his fate and even his death without complaint. That sacrifice not only makes him great, but it also opens up forgiveness for our sins.

Though there can be a way back, Isaiah understands that it is not something that will happen without sacrifice and a change of heart. God offers mercy, but people need to accept it. The message is straightforward: if you are thirsty, come and drink; if you are penniless, come and seek what you need. Change your thinking and find out how quickly God forgives.

After all the disputes with other nations, the most astonishing thing is that this offer is for everyone who wants it, no matter who they are, no matter where they come from. This will be a golden age as Jerusalem sparkles in the sun. It will be like the wedding of the century between God and his people with good news for the poor, release for the prisoners and healing for the brokenhearted.

Why not now?

The book closes as it opened, with the tensions and hopes still visible. 'Why don't you tear the sky in two and come down to us?' people ask God. Yet they go on ignoring him, not even bothering to pray. As God points out, if you want to be helped, at the very least, you have to ask.

In spite of every disappointment, God refuses to give up on his people. He will love them; he will comfort them and, one day, there will be a new heaven and a new earth where people will live as they were intended to live. It may not be soon but, for those who follow God, it will come.

Isaiah: the promises

Where darkness reigns, there will be light.
The blind will see; the deaf will hear;
the wild places will bloom with flowers
and the lion will lie down with the lamb.
I have called you, says the Lord.
Seek forgiveness; rise on wings like eagles;
run and you won't grow weary.
There is a road back from sorrow, if only you love me.

Jeremiah:
chaos creeps closer

This book covers events in Judah, down south, at a time when the country is threatened firstly by Assyria, then Egypt. Finally, Babylon invades and captures Jerusalem. Jeremiah isn't always chronological, but what is clear and easy to follow is that these are not the best of times… not even close.

Jeremiah – a less-than-happy prophet who got thrown into jail, threatened with execution and left to drown in mud at the bottom of a well. Even before that, he's not keen on being God's messenger. 'I'm too young,' he argues, 'I'm no good at public speaking, I'm…'

God stops him: 'You're scared. Don't be. I'll look after things. You will have my words and the power that will bring nations to their knees.' So the young prophet steps out and tells the people of Judah what's happening around them. People ignore God, yet listen to almost anyone else. It's like having a spring with the finest mineral water and choosing to drink from a muddy puddle.

God is hurt because he rescued them and found them somewhere safe, yet his reward is that they ruin the very land they were given. People may try to look innocent and say: 'You surely can't be angry with me – what have I done?' It won't work. Things must be worked at differently and honestly. If that happens, there is still mercy. At that point, doing what is right will come easily.

Gathering storms

A change of heart feels a long way off as storm clouds and war horses gather. Jeremiah knows what will happen and it's almost too much to bear. He challenges the nation to find him just one person who does the right thing.

Nobody steps forward. People are rich and bloated because they've stolen stuff. Those who are supposed to speak for God tell lies. Everyone follows their own silliness.

'Look at how the sea breaks on the shore,' says the prophet. 'The waves may roar and thunder, but then they drop back. The sand marks the boundary. That's how God makes things. But you break every boundary, ignore every rule.'

To make it worse, people don't see how serious it is. A deep wound is treated like a tiny scratch.

'If something is wrong, do you think religious services will put it right?' Jeremiah continues. 'Not a chance. Hear what God is saying. Be fair. Stop cheating each other. Treat life as valuable.'

Sadly, it doesn't get any better. People are polite and friendly, but they're not to be trusted. They're looking out for themselves, not for each other. A plot is hatched against Jeremiah's life which leaves him wondering why the wicked and dishonest seem to do so well.

He ends up wishing he'd never been born and telling God his enemies will see him dead before the almighty has done anything. God replies that the position of prophet is still available when he eventually gets it all out of his system and stops talking nonsense. At that point, he'll find the strength he needs.

Out of shape

Warnings are only part of the picture. There is also the promise that one day, things will be good again, if only people turn back to the one who created and saved them. I'm like the potter, God tells him. I try to shape my creation into something good, something useful. But if the clay refuses to work, then there is nothing that can be done for it.

Jeremiah's job doesn't get any easier. He faces the leaders and actually breaks a clay pot in front of them. As it shatters, he says: 'That is us, that's what it's going to be like: a total mess with no way of putting it all back together again.' The reward for his honesty is that he gets beaten up and chained to a wall.

So Jeremiah complains to God again: 'I've been tricked into a job where everyone laughs and thinks I'm stupid. Are trouble and misery all I'm going to get in my life?'

Now, no one may seem to be listening, but King Zedekiah knows who he wants to talk to when the enemy armies arrive. If he's hoping for a miracle, he's disappointed. There are two choices, he's told – surrender or slaughter. As for the palace, that will be burned to the ground.

The underlying problem has been justice: if leaders aren't fair, they can't expect a fair country. 'Protect those who get cheated,' says the Lord. 'Stand up for those who have no one to look out for them. And, if you reckon you can get away with what you get up to, think again. I'm not a god hidden in one or two small corners. I am everywhere.'

Easy words or tough truths?

Jeremiah warns the people that chaos is creeping closer. Some want him executed, but others reply that you don't kill prophets simply because what they say is tough. Naturally, there's always someone else to offer the comfortable messages that people want to hear.

Jeremiah is the one left to say: 'If you're in exile in Babylon, get on with it. Make the best of it, you'll be there quite a while… and pray for the people who have taken you prisoner.'

It's not all doom and gloom. There will be a day when people come home, when they dance again and wake up each morning feeling fantastic. First, though, there are the dark times. The fall of Jerusalem is bloody and brutal. Zedekiah sees his own sons publicly executed; then his eyes are gouged out and he's dragged away in chains. The most useful are taken to Babylon. Jeremiah is left behind and watches murderous power squabbles continue in the ruined land.

'Pray for us,' the people beg: 'Once there were so many, but now there are so few. Pray and ask what we should do.'

The answer from God is simple: if you are willing to live here, to work this land and to obey me, I will be with you and you need not fear your enemies. If you are tempted to give up and try your luck in Egypt, you won't return and you won't survive.

It's not what people want to hear, so many head west anyway. The problem isn't Egypt itself. It's that, when you leave home, you tend to leave your faith behind as well, go with the flow and forget the God who loves you.

The end

The bad news isn't restricted to one region. Moab, Ammon, Edom, Hazor and Damascus are also told they'll be overtaken by destruction. Walls will fall, people will scatter, only ruins will be left.

Even Babylon, which has wreaked all this havoc, will eventually be blown away like dry straw in the wind. No one is strong forever. Those who destroy will then be destroyed themselves. Jeremiah's vivid description of Babylon's collapse and his call to God's people to take the road home as soon as they can finishes what he has to say. That's followed by details of the fall of Jerusalem.

A key feature of the book is the realisation that, however weighed down you feel today, things will change. There's also much to learn about moaning. People may drag each other down with their misery, but God stands firm. When the complaints are over, he's there, waiting for us to rejoin the team that works for him. In God's world, you may be down, but you're never out.

Jeremiah's life lessons

- Mark the boundary between right and wrong – then stay the right side of it.
- Being polite and friendly doesn't make up for not looking after each other.
- If you let God shape the person you are, then something lovely will emerge.
- Be fair. Listen to God. Treat life as the treasure that it is.

Lamentations:
long time down

Five poems about life as it fell apart when Jerusalem was destroyed. A glimpse into how it felt to see the place in which you grew up wrecked and the people you loved taken away. The darkest of thoughts, lit up by brief moments of hope.

City of the lost

Jerusalem – how lonely the city seems now.
All night long the tears run down her cheeks;
every day she looks for friends but finds no one.
What happened to her people?
They were rounded up and dragged away,
encircled by enemies, no home and no escape.

The voices of the city are gone.
No one comes to worship.
Girls, who once sang, suffer in silence,
people trade treasure for food.

This place is burnt by the Lord's anger, eaten by a storm of fire.
All the wrong hangs upon her, drains her strength.
I stretch out my hands – but to whom?
There are no friends left
and, to my enemies, I'm a dirty rag in a forgotten corner.

It's not unfair, Lord, but look upon this agony,
for sins have crushed my heart.
When I go out, I see murder on the streets;
when I stay in, I smell death in every room.
Hear my voice and act against my enemies.
There is no one else to comfort me now.

Throwing darkness

Like a raging fire, he surged against us;
in his anger, he flung darkness on our lives;
like an enemy, the Lord marched through this land.
Nothing in the city is left standing;
the very gates lie buried in rubble.
We've lost the vision, the rules… even the way home.

How can I comfort anyone in this unending disaster?
People should have said what was wrong:
instead, they looked away.
Now nobody knows what is right anymore.

Look upon us:
young and old lie dead together in the street,
priests are murdered in the temple
and I have watched my children die.
Lord, you let our enemies do this to us
in a festival of horror, a carnival of slaughter.

Save me

How does it feel to be punished by God?
Like falling deep into darkness:
broken, beaten, bleeding.

Chained fast in my prison, I scream for help.
He isn't listening.
No hope and no escape – only walls on every side.

I am torn apart,
face rubbed in gravel until my teeth crack and break.
But the real bitterness and pain is that I have no home.

Only one thing gives me hope.
The Lord's love and mercy are not broken.
They rise, fresh as the dawn, sure as the sunrise.
What hope I have lies in him.

To those who trust, he is good.
Be patient; accept the bad times.
They will not last forever,
for God takes no pleasure in grief or pain.

We've deserved the insults, chaos, tears.
But, when I begged you to listen, you heard me,
you came to my rescue,
saved my life,
taught me to be afraid no more.
When you choose between me and my enemies,
Lord, choose me.

Wheel turning

We thought we were special;
we thought we could do what we liked.
We were wrong.

The golden children of Jerusalem, who feasted like kings,
now scrabble like animals amongst the rubbish.
Children beg for food,
babies die of hunger,
mothers no longer care.

It would have been better to be cut down in the war.
This is slow death: shrivelled, blackened, eaten by starvation.

We didn't believe it could happen, thought we'd be all right:
foolish… thoughtless… wrong.
That is why God scatters us.

People laugh at how we stumbled into disaster
but they will know what it feels like, too.
The wheel turns.
We have paid a price but this is not the end
and, one day, our exile will be over.

Bring us back

Is there no limit to your anger, Lord?
Look at us:
we pay for the water we drink and the fuel we need,
while strangers live in the houses we once owned.

Our fathers have been killed,
our wives and daughters raped,
our leaders hanged in public.

All we do is struggle like slaves
who stagger under loads,
plodding onward like beasts of burden.

The old no longer sit in corners to talk about life;
the young no longer gather to make music.
Where once we danced, now there are only tears.

What we treasured lies broken.
Why have you abandoned us?
Will you ever remember us?
Bring us back, Lord.
Or is there no limit to your anger?

Lamentations in short

The voices of Jerusalem are gone.
Where once we danced, now we sit and wait for death.
We thought we were special,
but we lost the line between right and wrong
and stumbled into a circus of chaos.
We deserve what we have got, Lord.
Only your love and mercy can save us now.

Ezekiel:
hard times but grand designs

This is a book that deals with exile in Babylon. The Jewish people were taken there from Jerusalem in at least two groups. It's not always clear exactly where Ezekiel was living at particular times, but that doesn't affect the things he has to say. What matters to Ezekiel is the thought that it's never too late to turn from evil. With God there is always hope.

When I was 30, explains Ezekiel, the sky opened. I was living with the exiles down by the river in Babylon. There was a wind storm, lightning flashed and four creatures appeared.

Ezekiel describes them as being like humans but with four wings, four hands and four faces. They glow and pass round a torch as an ice dome sparkles above them. Suddenly Ezekiel realises this isn't a bad dream, this is from God. So he bows to the ground.

God says: 'Don't do that; stand up. I want to talk to you.'

Ezekiel's task is to tell those in Jerusalem what a mess they've made, so it's no great surprise that Ezekiel isn't keen on the work. Nonetheless, he's soon dramatising his message by building a model of a city under siege and acting out what it will be like.

Theatre of the strange

Ezekiel's street theatre involves, among other things, lying on his left side for 390 days and cooking with cow dung. Not very attractive, but then neither is what's coming: war, disease, starvation, even people eating human flesh. The leaders are shaken and change their ways… for the moment, at least.

Sadly, it doesn't last, and a year later Ezekiel has a vision of Jerusalem with its temple shared by snake gods and sun worshippers. Frankly, it's not what God had in mind for his building.

Ezekiel acts out what it's like to be a refugee, digging through the wall of his house with his bare hands to make the point. The vivid warnings come thick and fast, but responses don't. The men talk up their own ideas rather than listening to God: it's like giving your house a coat of paint when the walls are collapsing. The women have a different approach: they make magic wristbands. No one is looking at the actual problems.

One day

This is a book of contrasts. In Jerusalem, where people blame their bad behaviour on others, the future looks stacked with death and destruction. In Babylon, God promises that, wherever his people are, he will be there as well. They have nowhere to call their own, but they can still worship God. He will hear them and, one day, he'll gather them back together again.

It isn't only the Jewish nations of Israel and Judah that are in trouble. Other lands are equally at fault, feeling that good looks and strength make them invulnerable. Finally, the day comes that Ezekiel has been dreading. A refugee escapes to bring the message that Jerusalem has fallen to invaders.

When your country lies wrecked, it's hard to hold on to the idea that the creator of the world still cares about you. So God shows Ezekiel a desert valley, full of bones dried out in the sun. 'Can these live?' asks God.

The answer should be 'no', but Ezekiel is used to strange happenings by now. 'It's up to you, Lord,' he replies. 'Only you can decide something like that.'

'All right,' declares God, 'tell these bones that they will live again.'

So Ezekiel speaks to the dead bones and they start coming to life until there's an army of people filled with God's Spirit.

'Everything feels like a dead end at the moment,' God tells his prophet, 'but I will breathe life into this barren wilderness and set you free. Then, when you return home, you are going to work together. No Israel in the north and Judah in the south: just one land, one people, one God.'

Grand designs

The promise is backed up by a vision of the new temple which Ezekiel sees as if he's flying high above it. Back at ground level, he gets the mathematics and technical detail.

This temple will be massive, a truly safe place for worship. But it will also have symmetry, a perfect square to match God's passion for equality and fairness. Not everyone is going to share this future. The dream is for those who are truly sorry for what has happened and want to worship together, at peace with God and with all their neighbours.

So the prophet becomes a one-man programme planner for a people who have experienced very little hope. He points to a future when they are home again, doing the right things and being fair to each other. And he sees them celebrating in a fabulous new temple with a special name, *Jehovah-Shammar*: the Lord is there.

Ezekiel: lessons from lives gone wrong

- People may make changes when challenged, but that doesn't mean those changes are going to last.

- When things go seriously awry, there's a worrying tendency to gloss over the underlying problems.

- If there's bad behaviour, the easy response is to blame it on other people.

- However desolate or desperate the future looks, God's Spirit can still breathe new life into the most unlikely places.

Home
Exile
Love
Faith
Home

Daniel:
dream central

Daniel is different. First, it was written bilingually – starting in Hebrew, switching to Aramaic and returning to Hebrew part way through. Second, it's a curious mixture of story, prophecy and strange dreams. This is about living honest, straightforward and wise lives. It's about people who are fearless when confronting corruption because they trust that their God will remain faithful.

Are you good-looking, intelligent and well-mannered? King Nebuchadnezzar needs you. This was the invitation that got Daniel into the royal palace and it takes a bit of explaining.

The Babylonian army has swept through Israel, overrun Jerusalem and taken people away as slaves. So why does the king of these marauding empire builders want to groom Jewish men like Daniel for possible high office? Because he collects ethnic influences to make his land ever more distinguished. Quite multicultural… in an odd sort of way.

Being yourself

Daniel seems happy enough to be one of those chosen. What he's not so willing to do is give up his identity. 'As Jews, we need to eat our own food,' he tells the head of the palace, 'not the royal menu.'

'I'd allow it,' the official tells him, 'but the king would kill me if you ate your own stuff and ended up looking worse than the others.'

'Trust me,' says Daniel. 'Let us live on vegetables and water for ten days. Then do a mirror test – us against the rest.' The result is a bit of a shock for meat eaters – vegetables make you look great.

Equally unexpected is that these young lads enjoy reading books. After three years, it's Daniel and his friends who stand out to the king. They're given top jobs and seem to know ten times more than the resident experts.

Dream nightmare

The first big test of their new status is Nebuchadnezzar's vision. The king has a palace full of sorcerers and wizards to help him with such things. One day, he becomes worried by a particular dream. But he's also bothered about the team who advise him.

'Interpret what I saw,' he tells them.

'Certainly,' they reply. 'What was it?'

'No,' says the king, 'tell me what the dream was and then what it means.'

'Umm… you need to tell us the dream first,' the advisers explain.

'Just as I thought,' growls the king. 'You're not magic at all. You'll be torn limb from limb.'

'But no one on earth can do what you're asking,' they complain.

'Off with their heads!' he roars.

The first that Daniel knows about this is when he discovers that his own head is one of those at risk. He sets up a prayer meeting, then gets a good night's sleep in which the puzzle of the king's dream is made clear to him.

'Thank you, Lord,' he declares. 'You're in charge of everything. I knew you'd give me the answer.' He doesn't say it but he probably thinks: 'And my head can stay attached to my shoulders.'

Daniel gets the executioner to take him to the king: 'Got one of the Jewish tribe here, your majesty. Reckons he can do the dream thing.'

'Well,' asks the king, 'Can you?'

'Not me,' answers Daniel, 'but God can and he wants me to tell you.'

The vision is about the future and the king is stunned by the detailed explanation he gets. Executions are off, replaced by a large promotion for Daniel at court, plus big local government posts for his friends Shadrach, Meshach and Abednego.

Burning issues

So far, so good. But things are never straightforward with Nebuchadnezzar.

'I want a statue,' he declares, 'in gold… of me.'

'About what size?' asks the builder.

'Twenty-seven metres high.'

When it's finished, there's a massive and glorious ceremony to celebrate. 'Now,' says the king, 'whenever the trumpets blow, you can bow down and worship me.' It isn't exactly compulsory… but the alternative is being burnt alive.

It's not a great situation for those who follow God, especially as there's always someone to tell on you. 'Your majesty,' say a couple of mealy-mouthed officials, 'you know those men you put in charge of our province – Shadrach, Meshach and Abednego? Well, they aren't doing what you told them to do; they don't bow to the statue.'

The king, as usual, loses his temper. 'Is it true?' he roars, when Daniel's friends are brought before him. 'Well, let's see if your god saves you now. Stoke up the furnace and throw them in.'

The guards get burnt alive, but the three friends can be seen walking in the heart of the fire with someone else. Nebuchadnezzar, who is watching, looks closely: 'The fourth one looks like a god,' he observes. For once, he's right.

So it's out of the fire and into promotions. There's also a recognition that the God they worship really is the one and only. By this stage, you may well be able to guess Nebuchadnezzar's punishment for anyone who disrespects God from now on. He threatens to have them torn limb from limb.

The king's second big dream also comes Daniel's way. Once again, God tells him the meaning. It's about the king's pride, which will be followed by seven years of madness. Daniel gets the message clearly enough but isn't keen to pass it on. Not surprising, really.

He gives the warning anyway and Nebuchadnezzar is reduced to roaming the fields, lost and alone. When the years of illness are over, it's a much-sobered king who admits that the praise and the glory belong to God, not to any of us.

The return of the dream solver

Belshazzar comes to the throne after Nebuchadnezzar. He knows how to throw a dinner party but not very much about God. In the middle of raising wine goblets to idols one night, a hand appears and writes on the palace wall: *mene, tekel, parsin.*

His special advisers have no idea what it means, but his mother knows what to do. 'Listen, son,' she says. 'We had a dream solver who was amazing at these mysteries. He's the one you want.'

The king calls for Daniel, who offers him a history lesson so he can understand what has gone wrong. Then he tells Belshazzar what the words mean: his days are numbered and his time is up; his work has been measured and it doesn't measure up; what he leaves behind will be carved up.

This king doesn't lose his temper and rewards Daniel for his insight, but he dies that very night and Darius, the Mede, seizes power.

The plot

Daniel becomes one of his three governors. Once again, he's good at his job: efficient, honest, reliable. People start wondering why all officials can't be like him. The other two governors don't appreciate that. They can't complain about Daniel's work so they find another way to get him.

This is their plot. They persuade Darius to sign an order so that, for 30 days, all requests must be addressed to the king. It sounds innocent enough, but this includes prayer requests. The punishment for offenders is a night with the lions, as an edible snack.

Of course, as the king is signing the order, he's not thinking about the consequences. Kings rarely do. When it's pointed out to him that Daniel is still praying to God and not even trying to hide the fact, the king's appalled – this isn't what he meant at all.

But government policy means that rules are rules and Daniel is chucked that evening into a pit of lions. The king doesn't eat, doesn't sleep. When it starts to get light, he hurries down to the lion's den. Daniel is unharmed.

'God looked after me,' he tells the king. Darius is delighted, gets Daniel pulled out of the pit and puts the two trouble-making governors in his place… just as the lions recover their appetites.

It's the end of Daniel's troubles because the king realises he has met a living God, someone who really can rescue people from the pits they create for themselves. Daniel has learned that, if you stick with God, it will work out one way or another.

Sleeping and rising

The later chapters of the book deal with Daniel's dreams. The first one involves four ugly beasts. One of them has great iron teeth to crush its victims and a talking horn with human eyes. The creatures, Daniel is told, stand for empires and they will all fall in time, even the most powerful of them.

The second vision involves a great ram that attacks anything until it's destroyed by a goat that then wrecks God's temple. It's a picture of the end of the world and of the destruction to come. Daniel hears what it means but can't say he really understands it.

In the midst of the dreams and their puzzles, Daniel prays because he knows what a mess his own people have made of everything. He's part of a generation that has taken no notice and has got what it deserved.

He prays for a new start back in the city from which they were taken. His answer is a visit from an angel who promises that God hears him, God loves him. There will be forgiveness and they will go home. It may not happen quickly, but the time will come.

The last visions take Daniel well into the future. In one, he hears how kings will rise and fall; in another, a voice knocks him unconscious. He feels he has no strength left but he's told: 'Do not be afraid, because God cares greatly for you.'

The end of the book deals with the end of time itself. There's trouble and chaos on nearly every corner but that's not the whole of it. Although there will be judgement, there will also be salvation.

Those who lead wisely will make the sky bright; those who teach clearly will shine like stars; those who have died will live again. That, he is told, includes you, Daniel. You'll die. Everybody does. But you will rise too. And, when every trouble is over, you'll be there.

Daniel in short

Eight dreams
Four friends
Six death sentences
Assorted lions
Three kings
One God – always

Hosea:
love never gives up

Hosea is the first of the minor prophets. They get that name not because they're less important, but because the books are shorter than the ones that have come before. Hosea is from the northern kingdom of Israel. After a period of stability and peace, the country has experienced several weak, short-lived kings and attacks from its stronger neighbour, Assyria. It's a story from the last years of chaos before the people were taken into exile, but with a truth beyond time.

There are times when we love and the love is not returned. It's heartbreaking but it happens. That makes the love at the heart of what God does both unexpected and remarkable. He loves, even when there seems to be no purpose, no possible return. And this book spells it out.

Coming apart at the seams

Hosea marries Gomer who bears him two sons and a daughter. But she doesn't love him or, if she does, she loves plenty of others too. Gomer forgets how much Hosea has given her and his fury makes him think about ways of stopping her slipping away with other men. The children become messengers between the troubled parents. His anger burns, threats are muttered, but nothing changes.

Just as it is between Hosea and Gomer, so it is between God and his people: things have fallen apart. It was different when the nation escaped from slavery in Egypt. Love was young then. But age need not wither feelings. It's a matter of going back to where it all began, recognising how you came through the troubles together and opening a door marked 'hope'. This is love for those who feel unloved, a voice that is the same yesterday, today and forever. It is God's promise that you are his permanently.

In our world, even if we feel we can rely on God, there's still the challenge of people who let us down. Keep loving Gomer, God tells Hosea. And he does, paying off her debts and waiting for her, just as God waits for us.

But the problems that this prophet sees are wider than one person. So much has come adrift in the northern kingdom where he lives. People make promises but they don't keep them: they steal, they sleep around and crime increases as murder follows murder.

Delete religion, insert faith

The ones who are most to blame are the leaders who are too busy chasing more money and other ways of believing. What do you expect, asks God, if you seek revelation from a piece of wood? That's not real faith, it's just an excuse to make up what people want to hear.

What's happening is so bad, warns Hosea, that the signposts for life have disappeared entirely. God warns them and appears to get a response.

'Let's return to the Lord,' they say. 'He's hurt us but he'll surely heal us, and in a couple of days we can live comfortably in his presence again.'

'I don't want any more religious services,' God tells them, 'I want your constant love. I don't want your sacrifices, I want you.'

It's as if the people imagine they're invisible to God. When they should be praying, they're fixing up military deals. Even that they do badly. 'If you sow the wind,' says God, 'you'll reap the whirlwind.'

If they seek me

There was something special when God called them and Moses led them out of Egypt. They were like grapes growing in the desert, but faith is now dried up and lifeless. So their future will be in exile in Babylon, far from home, where they'll just have to survive as best they can.

In all this tangled mess, one thing remains. God still cares for them. 'When the nation was young I loved it as a child,' he recalls, 'I took these people in my arms, held them to my cheek, fed them when they were hungry.'

He cannot save them from the consequences of their behaviour, but he cannot give up on them. They can lie, they can cheat, they can be hopelessly evil in dozens of ways, but his heart will not allow him to turn away totally. God longs for them to remember that at the end of all things, only he is there.

People disappear like morning mist; idols come and go; only God stays the same. There can be no pity if no one turns to him but, if only they would, the promise is new life.

'I will bring my people back to me,' declares God, 'I will love them with all my heart. I will be like the rain that makes the trees grow and the flowers bloom. If their prayers are for me, my answers will be for them; if they seek me, I will shelter them and bless them.'

There's a warning alongside the promise: those who ignore the message will stumble and fall. So the prophet ends by asking his listeners to do two simple things: hear the wisdom of love and take it to heart.

Hosea: constant in love

Love that was young once changes in time
but age need not wither it.
God's promises remain the same;
his love for the unloved never wavers.
At the end of all things he is there:
he will bring his people back.
If they seek him, he will shelter them,
bless them and cradle them in his arms.
God can be trusted for all of that.
The question is: can they be trustworthy too?

Joel:
back from the edge

Locusts, droughts, dreams and turning back to God: that's what Joel covers as he responds to a national crisis. Apart from the fact that his father is named Pethuel, we know nothing for sure about him or the time at which he lived. What we do learn is that, in the middle of a disaster, there's a need to both take personal responsibility and to seek God.

Joel says: listen up. Has anything like this happened before? One swarm of locusts follows another like fire scorching the garden of Eden. The earth shakes and the skies tremble. It's like an army that crawls over everything. They crackle like burning grass, rattle like chariots in full flight, arrive like a black cloud sweeping down from the mountain. Nothing stops them, nothing holds them up. And, when they're through, paradise has been replaced by desert. No figs, no grapes, no olives, no grain. Not even seed so you can start again.

What on earth do you make of such devastation? Joel believes he knows: God is telling us to turn back to him. He needs people who are heartily sorry for what they've done wrong, not just the ones who act as if they are.

'Come together in prayer,' he tells them. 'God is kind and loves to be merciful. He's the promise-keeper who is always more ready to forgive than to punish. Perhaps our devastated world can start again with a new harvest and we'll have gifts of food to offer God once more.'

The prophet's words hit home and, as the people show they're sorry for what has gone wrong, God responds: 'I will give you corn and wine and oil, I'll drive the locusts from your land. I will make the fields green and the trees full of fruit again. The rains will come when you need them and the harvests will overflow. Then you will know that I am your God and no one else can take that place.'

Spirit dreams

It sounds like a good enough place for a book to finish, but Joel looks further into the future to see something altogether greater.

'Your sons and daughters will be filled with my message,' God promises. 'Young men will see visions, old men will dream dreams. You may be at the bottom of the pile and think that you don't count for very much but it's not true. I will pour my Spirit out on you.'

The time of dreams will also be a time when people face up to consequences. God will roar like a mountain lion against anyone who has abused their position and taken what isn't theirs. Those who have stayed faithful will find something quite different: a place to live quietly, where the waters flow, the crops grow and God can be worshipped in peace.

Disasters, warnings, visions and promises are standard ingredients for a prophet. But one thing marks Joel out from the rest. He saw a spirit coming that didn't recognise any difference between men and women, young and old, rich and poor. Not bad for a book that starts with a sky full of locusts.

Three questions from Joel

- When paradise turns into desert, are you ready to wonder if it's your fault?
- When you say you're sorry, do you actually mean it?
- If you have a dream, are you willing to follow it?

Amos:
not expected, not wanted

Amos was a small businessman who saw what happened across the land in which he lived and traded. The rich seemed to believe wealth was a reward from God for worshipping properly. It didn't occur to them that they might be rich because they paid the poor so badly. Amos puts them right.

A man stands up and shouts at the people who have turned up for worship: 'I can't stand it anymore. All this singing, praying and preaching: it makes me feel sick.'

Awkward enough in any situation, but particularly troublesome if the man who's standing up is God. Just one of the many difficult thoughts you can find in Amos, the earliest recorded prophet in the Bible. He's not an obvious choice for this kind of work: a sheep farmer from Judah in the south, attempting to sort out Israel in the north. Not what anyone probably expected… or wanted.

Fish on hooks

The messages actually start quite nicely for Israel, because Amos delivers judgements on everyone else first. The nations around them have broken treaties, turned neighbours into slaves, even trampled over people with spiked logs. Storms of fire are coming to sort out these enemies of God. His listeners are probably thinking, 'Good enough for them.' Then the messages that started with Syria creep closer until Amos is talking about his own land of Judah, next door. You can see what's coming next.

Those people, who have been taking it all in and nodding smugly, suddenly find the spotlight turned on them. Things may look all right at your religious services, Amos tells them, but your lives are horribly wrong. You take advantage of someone who owes you next to nothing; you rip the clothes off people's backs as security for debts. You were given so much, but you give back so little.

Israel has become the essence of indulgence: where the rich have fabulous homes, filled with stuff they've got through crooked dealing and squeezing every last penny out of the poor. The feel-good days of fine dining, endless wine and fabulous music are numbered. The day is coming, says God, when the people who do nothing but enjoy themselves are dragged away like fish on hooks.

Surely not me

The pattern of people's lives is clear. Go to worship. Return home and forget all about everyone else. Pray with others. Go back and lose yourself in luxury. Give money to good causes. Continue doing exactly what you like.

You've had drought and disease and food shortage, observes God. Didn't you get the hint that not everything was right? You saw troubles and did nothing.

So God can't bear to hear their worship anymore. It's just infuriating. 'Stop doing religion and start doing fairness,' is the message. 'Hate what is evil. Love what is right. Let justice flow like a river that never runs dry.'

As the people keep denying there's a problem, this doesn't look likely. The people have let justice become poisoned. That's about as sensible as trying to plough the oceans with oxen. What's worse – they don't even notice it.

Amos dreams that locusts swarm down just as the harvest starts and that fires burn so hot that the sea itself dries up. He asks God to hold back and the Lord hears him. But the third vision shows him that this can't go on forever. Amos sees God as a builder checking a wall which isn't straight. There's no getting away from it: the wall is crooked and so are the people.

Bad and good

It's at about this time that the leaders decide they want a more positive message. Amos is told to make money in his own country and leave them alone. 'I don't do this for cash,' he replies. 'I actually run a sheep business… plus I've got a few fig trees. I do this because I have to – for God. Getting rid of me doesn't get rid of the bad news.'

A dream about ripe fruit is a warning that the people will be swallowed up, but even as disaster looms they're focused on profit margins. Of course, when everything comes crashing down, they'll suddenly go searching for the God they've been ignoring. The trouble is, that will be too late.

In the final vision, Amos sees God in the temple at Bethel. It's gone so wrong that he's breaking up the building himself. The earth's being shaken and no one can hide, no one can escape. Those who thought, 'It can never happen to us,' are discovering that it can.

You might expect Amos to end there, but it doesn't. Because ruins can be repaired, walls can be rebuilt, a people can be restored. Then the corn will grow freely, the mountains will flow with sweet wine and the people will live once more with God in their own land.

The comfort of the final words doesn't take away the thought that it didn't actually have to get so bad in the first place. If only people had lived out the words they said in worship, this book would never have been needed.

Amos: what religion isn't

Religion isn't there to make you feel comfortable or excuse your greed. It isn't there so you can forget about others and live in luxury. God wants all that's right and fair flowing like a river that never runs dry. Religion isn't about profit margins; it's about listening to the prophet.

Obadiah:
family fallout

A short book with a long history. Jacob and Esau were brothers whose families set up the nations of Israel and Edom. They fell out so badly that, when Babylon's army trashed Israel's capital, Jerusalem, the people of Edom helped the enemy and took what they could from the wreckage. This is what Obadiah is talking about.

Obadiah says: you think you're strong because the mountains where you live look like a rock-solid defence. You're wrong. Home can be as high as an eagle's nest, but God can still pull it down. Thieves only take what they want; harvesters always leave a little behind. But you are going to be picked so clean that nothing is left. And it will be your old friends who trap you and drive you out.

Why will this happen? Because you saw what was going on with your relatives and you did nothing. You shouldn't just have stood by and watched; you shouldn't have enjoyed their misery. Then, when the fighting stopped, you shouldn't have stolen what was left and sneered at their suffering. When the refugees were escaping, you should never have betrayed them to their enemies.

What you did to others will be done to you– and worse. You will vanish without trace. But the people you scorned will return and the mountains will be ruled justly as part of God's own country.

Obadiah in a sentence

Whatever you think of your family, however much you've fallen out with them, that's never an excuse to be cruel.

Jonah:
a whale of a time

Jonah is a successful prophet in Israel by the time of the story in this book. He features in 2 Kings as a bringer of good news. However, delivering a message to the most feared empire on earth is a challenge of a vastly different order. This isn't about how you behave with friends but what you do about enemies.

Jonah's story starts simply enough. God gives his prophet a job: 'Get down to Nineveh and tell them that the evil has to stop.'

It sounds straightforward, but it isn't. The city is the heart of the Assyrian Empire, feared for its power, its cruelty and its skills in torture. Being a friend or ally of these people made good sense. Telling them they were wrong meant risking life and limb.

Wrong direction

To follow God's request, Jonah should have gone east by land. Instead, he heads west by sea to Tarshish in Spain. That's about 3,000 miles away from Nineveh. Jonah seems to be choosing sand and sunshine, rather than risking life and limb.

Bad choice. The weather's fine as the boat leaves the harbour, but it doesn't last. Jonah is asleep when the captain bursts in. 'How can you sleep in a storm like this?' he yells. 'Start praying.'

As sailors blame bad weather on bad people, they draw lots to find out who's to blame. Jonah gets the short straw. 'Who are you?' they ask, 'and what on earth are you doing here?'

'I've run away,' Jonah tells them, 'from God.'

The storm goes on growing and the sailors are terrified. 'What are we going to do?' they cry.

'Get rid of me,' says Jonah. 'Chuck me in the sea.'

Of course, crews don't much like losing their passengers so they make one final massive effort to get to shore. Useless! Then, praying they won't be punished, they heave Jonah over the side.

Second chances

Peace out of chaos. The waves ease almost immediately. And Jonah? Nowhere to be seen. He's been swallowed by a big fish, which most people understandably reckon to be a whale. All that Jonah knows is that he's trapped for three days and nights in a living grave, choked with salt water and draped in seaweed.

So, he does what he should have done in the first place and prays to God:

I'm in deepest, darkest trouble, Lord,
I feel like I've been thrown away.
Help me, save me
and I will keep my promise to you.

God hears his distress and gives him a second chance. The creature vomits and Jonah finds himself on dry land again. That, however, takes him back to square one. God hasn't changed his mind. It's still a case of: Nineveh – message – you.

So Jonah does what God wants. On arrival, he starts going through the city and finally he delivers his warning: 'Forty days are left – then Nineveh will be destroyed.'

Given their terrifying reputation, you'd expect this lot to provide Jonah with a thorough beating at best. But guilt's a funny business – the smallest thing can trigger it. The people know they deserve no better than meltdown and they not only feel guilty but admit to it too. Even more astonishingly, they start to change their ways, the king included, and they ask God to relent.

God is delighted and opts for mercy rather than punishment. Jonah is furious: he's the prophet whose prophecy hasn't happened. 'See,' he tells God, 'this is why I didn't want to come. You're patient, kind, always ready to listen. I knew this would happen. I just wish I was dead.'

How God cares

Jonah heads out east of the city and builds a shelter to wait and see what happens next. God makes a leafy plant grow up over him which gives him shade from the desert sun and cheers him up. The next day it withers and Jonah finds himself caught in the burning heat of the day. He's furious about the withered plant. 'I'd be better off dead than alive,' he declares.

God asks him: 'What's all this anger about? You are sitting here caring about a plant that sprang up overnight and has now died. Shouldn't I care about those in Nineveh who still have much to learn?'

Jonah: in the end

This is the only book among the prophets to end with a question. It doesn't record Jonah's answer or even if he gave one. There isn't a single word on what he did next. Perhaps that's because this is not essentially about what prophets do. Maybe, it's actually about how far we reflect God's kindness of heart. Do we care about the little things that make us comfortable or the big things that really matter? Do we like to see bad people getting what they deserve or can we show them kindness? And, as Jonah discovered, sometimes the journey you need to take isn't the journey you want.

Micah:
all that lies ahead

Micah was a southern prophet from a small, out-of-the-way town who didn't much like what he saw, particularly in the city. He lived at the same time as Isaiah. Both prophets were shocked by Jerusalem and how those in power took advantage of their position. The land was under threat at this time from the Assyrian army and, in 734BC, much of the country fell into their hands.

'Listen,' Micah says, 'I will walk barefoot and naked. I will howl like a wild animal because of what happens here. You make dozens of alternatives to God and there are temples making money from prostitution. This is so wrong.

'You know about God but you ignore him. The Lord is coming to get rid of all this, striding down from the mountains as everything melts in his tracks like wax in a fire.

'The trouble with sin is that it's like a virus which spreads everywhere. Those who lead you now will soon be hiding in caves just to stay alive. And those who cheat others will actually come off worse. When it's all put right, there will be no share for those who have never shared.'

Naturally enough, Micah isn't popular with everyone. 'Don't be so preachy,' people tell him, 'or so gloomy. God isn't really going to do those things to us.'

Micah's response is simple. 'Don't think God will keep you safe from your enemies. You're the ones who drive people from their homes and take the coats from off their backs. You *are* the enemy.'

Not all bad… but mostly

It's not, of course, a message to every single person. Although destruction and exile are looming, God will gather his people back together one day. He will open a way and they will return to the land where they belong.

What makes the current situation so bad is that those in charge prefer evil to good. 'You're skinning my people alive!' shouts Micah. 'You're breaking every bone in their bodies and serving them up for lunch.'

Even the other prophets are not to be trusted. Micah points out that, if you give them money, then they'll make reassuring noises about peace. If you don't, they'll mutter darkly about war.

'Listen to me,' he says, 'because I'm telling it to you straight from God. You can't build a future with injustice; you can't create a strong world when people just give the answers you want.'

A backwater son

That's the news for today. But Micah doesn't leave it there. 'In days to come,' he promises, 'there will be peace as people turn to God, learn from him and follow his paths.

'Nations will hammer swords into ploughs and spears into pruning hooks. God will settle the disputes between peoples and they will never prepare for war again. The time for this is getting nearer but it isn't yet. There's pain to come but don't be misled by it.'

Where will this change start? A tiny backwater town on one of the trade routes: Bethlehem. 'Out of you,' Micah promises, 'will come a new ruler whose family line goes back deep into our history. The Lord will leave his people alone until the one who is to give birth produces a son. Then those who have been exiled will be reunited in a kingdom with its heart set on God and surrounded by peace.'

Micah's message has one basic contrast: people living with God versus people living in the strength of their own ideas. Those who depend on God will be like summer rain that lets the plants grow again; those who go their own way will be sleepwalking into total destruction.

Unquenchable love

God is astonished at how people ignore him. 'What have I done to you?' he asks. 'How have I been a burden? When you needed me, I was always there to rescue you.'

Love like that needs a response, but Micah makes clear it's not about turning up with expensive gifts. 'What God requires is that we do what is fair, go on loving each other and live quietly within his almighty arms.'

It sounds so easy, but Micah just can't find the people who will do such a simple, honest thing. Instead, he uncovers experts in evil who can't even be trusted by their friends and family.

If the book ended there, it would be a bleak story. But it doesn't. 'We have fallen,' says the prophet, 'but we will rise; we are in darkness now, but the light will shine. The Lord will see to it like a shepherd who finds good places for his flock. He does not stay angry forever; he is merciful and will get rid of the mess we have made. Then, all that lies ahead will be faithfulness and unquenchable love.'

Micah: warnings and promises

Don't expect a share if you've never shared yourself. Don't look for the enemy when, in fact, it's you. Don't believe the comforting things people tell you if you pay their wages. But do understand that peace will come as people turn to God. Those who fought as enemies will bring the harvest in together. And where will this change begin? In a small town called Bethlehem, where into darkness, a light will shine.

Nahum:
it's over

Nahum means 'comforter', but what he has to say includes some distinctly uncomfortable truths. The situation is this. Nineveh, the city that Jonah visited, has gone back to its very worst lifestyle. Back in Jonah's time, people changed their ways and found mercy. This time it's different.

God is good, a safe place in troubled times, but he's not there so you can just mess about and do what you like. Where the Lord walks, the weather turns wild. If he tells the rivers or the seas to dry up, that's exactly what they do. Mountains shake; hills melt; rocks crumble. The city of Nineveh may look strong, but its wealth and wild living won't survive. This is the final chapter. The hole that people are digging is their own grave.

What's coming

The messenger on the horizon is bringing good news and the promise of peace for those who follow God. But it's not for the ones who have totally ignored God, relying instead on brutal power and endless cruelty.

Enemies in red will attack those who have made others suffer. Chariots will flash like lightning through the sky. Suddenly, it will be too late. Those who were defending the city will be rushing to get out of it.

What was once the safest place in the world will be ripped apart in a scramble for its silver and gold. The city of killers will be dead itself: corpses piled high and people stumbling around the bodies.

The place may look great, but take away its sweet-talking, fashionable ways and suddenly there will be nothing left. Just tourists staring at ruins. Nineveh has more traders chasing business than there are stars in the sky, but when the bad times come, they'll have vanished. All that will be left is people cheering the city's disappearance.

Nahum: three warnings

- What was once a safe highway will become a street of corpses.

- What once sparkled fashionably will lie crumbled and ruined.

- A safe place in trouble is not built with money and wild parties but out of God's goodness and peace.

Habakkuk:
wheels turning

Habakkuk dates from about the same time as Jeremiah, when it looked as if Judah was about to be overrun. The book is a conversation between the prophet and God, ending with a poem that was turned into a song. So, in theory, you could read it, then strum it.

Habakkuk's first question for God is simple. How long can the current political mess possibly continue? The country is a disaster zone: the courts are useless, violence is everywhere and bad people just gobble up all the good stuff for themselves.

The answer is that this is about to change. 'You see those Babylonians,' says God, 'the ones with the fast horses who steal everything? Well, they're on their way. They're a law unto themselves. And, yes, they do believe in a god: it's called power.'

Tell me why

Habakkuk is astonished. So his second question is: 'Why them?' Surely the Lord isn't going to tolerate the behaviour of international hooligans. In answer, the prophet is directed away from the present towards what is to come.

Those who stay with God will continue to have their lives lit by faith and those who feel superior now will discover how their lives have gone rotten. The wheel turns, and wealth eats up those who have hungered for it.

The messages are blunt: if you build a city on crime, it burns; if you hurt and humiliate those around you, that is what you get, too. If you stash the cash, you can expect nothing from it. Things you buy or make, however expensive, are just things. They don't live and breathe, they're not your friends.

Even now

It's not exactly an answer for their problems, but Habakkuk understands that it is enough. 'Lord, I have heard you,' he says, 'and it stops me in my tracks. You have helped us before, so I trust you to do it again. Even when you are angry, remember to be merciful. I know you will show your strength, striding from the mountains as the skies blaze, riding the storm clouds as the earth shakes, striking down those who make others suffer, coming to save your people.'

It's not easy for the prophet. He admits his body shudders when he thinks about what they're facing. But, having seen the future, he waits quietly for what he knows will come and sings this:

Even though the fig trees do not blossom
and no grapes are upon the vine,
even though the olives do not grow
and the fields produce no food,
yet I will sing with joy
and be glad in God who saves me.
Wherever I may go, he will keep me safe
and make my footsteps sure.

What Habakkuk learnt

Bad things happen. Sometimes the hooligans take over the country. And it may actually be the selfishness of the people who live there that helps this to occur. But the wheel turns and, wherever you walk, God walks with you.

Zephaniah:
not just all the others

Zephaniah's great-great-grandfather was King Hezekiah, an outstanding leader from the southern territory of Judah. By the time Zephaniah was writing, things had gone seriously adrift in the land. However, the book dates from the later time of King Josiah, who became one of the country's great reformers. So, it's quite possible that what Zephaniah had to say actually did its work.

What bad men and women do tends to catch up with them, so Zephaniah's warning about a day when God sorts out wickedness sounds like good news for religious people. But it's not, because religious people are part of the problem. They talk about faith, then do what they like. That's a path to nowhere. They've become smug, thinking that God doesn't mind, but their cosy world is about to disintegrate.

'See those houses being built?' says the prophet. 'You'll never live in them. See those vineyards being planted? You'll never drink a drop of wine from them.'

The appeal is blunt: wake-up before you wither like flowers; turn back to God and do what is right.

The silence of ruins

Neighbouring countries are no better. Their destruction will be sudden and complete. Bustling towns will become silent; great farms will lie empty; big cities will be overgrown with weeds. If you're looking for the local council, they won't even be there. All you'll see is a wild animal staring back at you from among the ruins.

Those who should have spoken up did nothing; those who knew about God forgot every lesson they were taught. Now a fire will burn across the lands.

In spite of this, not everything will be lost. Each morning, as certain as sunrise, God will still be there. He will hear the ones whom others thought were unimportant, the ones who are honest about their faults, the ones who pray to him and call out for help.

Still there's joy

For all the dark talk of evil and its consequences, the book finishes with a song of praise. 'Let's hear your voices,' says Zephaniah. 'Let loose the joy that is in your heart because God is with you. He delights in you and brings new life. Fear has departed, for the nightmare days are over.'

God is coming to make life good again, to call his people home.

Zephaniah in a nutshell

- Talk about faith, yet do what you like? That's the problem.
- Smug and sure that God's fine with your behaviour? That's the road to disaster.
- Need to speak up but choose to keep quiet? That lets trouble run riot.
- Instead, let God fill your heart with joy and feel life begin anew.

Haggai:
halfway is nowhere

There's a lot in the Old Testament on the threat to Jerusalem, its destruction and the exile of people as slaves. Haggai was one of those who was in exile but who returned home for the rebuilding of the city. This book should be full of good news and hope, but what you think will happen isn't always what does.

The message delivered by Haggai is this: you came home from exile with such hope and you rebuilt your houses really well. But the temple is a wreck and all you can say is that it doesn't feel like the right time to work on it. Are you surprised that things aren't going well? People work on their own places but no one works on God's place. It's no wonder that life doesn't feel good. The easy tasks get done; the toughest challenges are left alone.

Got to get on with it

The prophet's words have the desired effect and the people make a start on their temple. It can't have been easy – the building was never popular with other people who lived in the area. But Haggai tells them that the message from God is simple: 'I will be with you.'

This is one of those occasions when everyone gets involved. As a result, the project goes well. Later that year, the prophet is encouraging them to finish what they've started. 'Can anyone remember how splendid the old building was? This time, it looks twice as good.' God is telling them not to be afraid, to keep going as they walk the road with him.

The book finishes with a report that God approves of the new governor, Zerubbabel, and a warning that something has got in the way of finishing the building project. It's not clear what the problem is but the solution is to make a change, say sorry, start again. That's the route from repeated frustration to true hope.

'We're disappointed now,' says the prophet: 'no grapes, no olives, no figs… but they will come. That's a promise. With the people in the right place with God, the world will be fruitful again.'

Haggai in a breath

- Do the difficult things as well as the stuff you like.

- Do it together.

- And keep going because you're walking with God.

- When things go wrong, say sorry, start again.

- It may not always look like it but you'll get there.

Zechariah:
endings and beginnings

Zechariah was a prophet who returned from exile about the same time as Haggai and faced a similar situation. It was good to be back, but there was still so much to be done. The book offers several visions of better days and of a leader who will come and make a difference – not like a king might, but like someone who is willing to suffer in order to rescue you.

'Your parents, your grandparents and your great-grandparents drove me mad with the way they behaved,' says God, 'but that doesn't mean that *you* have to do the same. Return to me and I will return to you.'

That's Zechariah's starting point among the wreckage of what was once a great city. The book is a mixture of warnings and promises for a people short on hope and it's fuelled by the strangest of dreams.

The visions

First up: a rider on a red horse meets three others under the myrtle trees. They've been travelling the world and things are calm, under control. This is followed by four ox horns and four blacksmiths. An angel explains that God's people may have been scattered in the past, but their enemies are no longer as strong as they once had been and it's time to rebuild.

Next into view is someone measuring Jerusalem. As one angel leaves, another arrives: 'No point in planning for new walls,' the angel comments, 'it's going to be far too big for that.' And the walls aren't needed anyway because God will protect the city. Jerusalem is suddenly going to be the place to be seen.

Another vision shows Joshua, the high priest, in filthy clothes with Satan stood next to him getting ready to bring accusations. Then God steps forward with this command: 'Give my priest a new set of clothes because he's been forgiven.' Change is taking place. It's a new-start day in a new-start city, where people work with one heart and mind.

After that, Zechariah sees a lampstand with seven lights alongside two olive trees. The picture is a puzzle but the message is made clear: it's not your strength that will make things happen but God's spirit. Barriers as big as mountains will disappear and the temple will rise again. When the last stone is placed in the last wall, you'll whisper, 'Oh, that's beautiful.' It doesn't look like it now but, bit by bit, this will happen.

A vision of a flying scroll is a warning to those who lie or steal. Then a woman is lifted out of the country – a sign that sins are being taken away and people can begin building with a clean slate. Finally, four chariots search the world to report back that troubled times have passed and Joshua is confirmed as the one who will make politics and religion work together.

Detail is an excuse

After the visions, some people have a curious question for Zechariah: 'Should we continue to fast in the fifth month in recognition of the temple's destruction?' It sounds rather holy and serious but it isn't.

'You like religious detail,' the prophet tells them, 'but God wants kindness and mercy. Be fair to each other and look out for those who aren't in good shape. These things have been ignored and that's how it went wrong in the first place.'

Nonetheless, God still loves Jerusalem and its people. There can be a future where children play safely in the streets while old men and women sit in the shade on sunny days. They can't imagine it, just now, but God specialises in the impossible.

'I will rescue my people,' he promises, 'and bring them back to an age of peace, rebuilding and good harvests. Trust me. Stop harming each other. Start putting peace and truth at the top of your to-do list.'

Someone's coming

'Look,' says Zechariah, 'your king is coming but not in the way you dreamed. He's on a young donkey, a peacemaker not a warrior. Exiles will return, and he'll be their shepherd. You don't need fortune-tellers. Alternative gods are useless. If you need something in this world, ask the person who made the planet.'

The prophet acts out one scene where a fake shepherd leaves his sheep to be butchered and another where the people go on ignoring the real shepherd for so long that he doesn't want the job anymore.

The book moves towards its ending with a mixture of troubles and triumphs. Jerusalem will be attacked, but its enemies will be destroyed. Anything that builds a wall between God and his people will be taken away. Prophets will be redundant because people will be listening directly to God.

In this future time, Zechariah sees a shepherd wounded, sheep scattered, violence, robbery, rape. People will flee in all directions as if an earthquake has struck. Then a plague will strike their enemies so that flesh rots on their bones, eyes rot in their sockets and tongues rot in their mouths.

Eventually, the prophet believes the ugliness will end in Jerusalem's renewed commitment to God. Troubles will be past and what lies ahead will be a world where people stay right with God: like looking towards the end and seeing the beginning again.

Zechariah: what the future holds

- Chaos doesn't last forever – a time to rebuild will come.

- You are not as strong as you think you are… but God is.

- Your failures can be forgiven: God is in the business of new hearts and starts.

- There will be a new world without barriers between you and God or each other.

- Someone is coming to make this possible and it's not who you expect.

Malachi:
turn to God

Malachi lived at roughly the same time as Ezra and Nehemiah. God's people have returned from exile to Jerusalem but the business of getting comfortable back home seems to have taken their minds in entirely the wrong direction.

God's people are back where they belong. The temple is rebuilt; worship is up and running. Everything should be starry-eyed and shining. But it's not.

'The problem is this,' says God. 'I have loved you and you don't appreciate it. See how much better you've done than those who didn't follow me. Then look at what you give back… it's rubbish. You've actually picked out what you don't want as a gift to me!

'Lock the doors of your temple, stop wasting your time in worship. If you can't do it properly, don't do it at all. Without big changes, blessings will become curses, until it feels like your face is being rubbed in a dung heap. It shouldn't be like that. I want to give you the full life people had way back when they lived in harmony with me.'

Bad for good

People don't even give each other a fair chance anymore. 'Don't we all have the same Father God?' Malachi asks. 'Didn't he create every one of us? So why do we do whatever we like when we could be faithful to him and to those we love? It's no good asking God why things are wrong in your world. You act as if bad is good and he's tired of it.

'Someone is coming who will prepare the way, like a fire that separates good metal from bad. You'll not be able to play fast and loose… in marriage, at work, anywhere. It is God you've been trying to cheat and you can't. Change this now, live fairly, give God what is due. The windows of heaven can still be opened to you. You complain that your work isn't appreciated and that bad people seem to get away with it. Think again.'

Standing in the sunshine

That's Malachi's message: short, punchy, challenging. Not everyone responded, but some stopped in their tracks and turned back to God. They are promised a time when all that's wrong will shrivel and die. Those who have been faithful will stand in the sunshine, feeling its warmth lift away every ache and pain.

Malachi ends by declaring that the prophet Elijah will be heard again, not returning to announce doom and gloom but to sort things out, to put relationships right and to see that families love each other better.

Malachi in a minute

- Don't moan about the problem. You are the problem.
- Live fairly; straighten yourself out.
- Someone is coming who knows the difference between bad and good.

So the Old Testament finishes and 400 years go by. Then Mark, the earliest of the gospel writers, picks up his pen and starts with a man in the desert whom people are calling the new Elijah. Faith and hope are in the air again, for the old story suddenly has a new voice.

NEW TESTAMENT

A word about the gospels

The story of Jesus, told four ways in Matthew, Mark, Luke and John, starts the New Testament.

Mark was almost certainly the first gospel to be written and it seems to have been done in a hurry. It makes sense to read the straightforward run-through of Mark first of all. This includes some brief background to help you understand why people think it was written in the way it was.

Much of Matthew and Luke are based around the same stories found in Mark. The story is told each time but the focus here is on the additional material they used and what makes these books distinctive.

John doesn't base stories around those found in Mark in any direct way, but offers a different perspective. As with Matthew and Luke, the account here tries to capture something of what is special about the gospel.

In theory, you could argue that you only need one clear accurate account of the life of Jesus. But then you'd lose the richness and the challenge of the different perspectives. The best way to find out about Jesus was, of course, to be there at the time. The best alternative is to have several accounts that can live side by side. Good news about the good news!

Matthew:
good news in the family

One of the things people often ask is whether Jesus actually existed at all. It's a fair question, but no one seems to have asked it back at the start. Critics complained that he was a magician and was leading people astray, but the fact he existed was never challenged. There are records of his life in Josephus, Pliny and Tacitus. Another reference dates back to just 20 years after his crucifixion. And Matthew decides to make the plain fact of his life clear by starting with details of his ancestry.

A family tree from Abraham to David to Jesus starts this book, followed by the story of the one who was expected but whose arrival was a surprise, potentially a scandal. You see, Mary is pregnant, and questions are being asked about who's the father. Not Joseph, who she's supposed to be marrying, but a power called 'the Holy Spirit' which will bring God among us. Now Joseph might have given several responses to that, but God's voice calls him in his dreams. 'Marry her,' it says, and he does.

When Jesus is born in Bethlehem, wise men from the east are led by a star to visit him. They bring gifts of gold, frankincense and myrrh but trouble as well. On their journey, they've stopped by King Herod's palace and asked about the birth of a new king. Not a bright idea when you're talking to a regular psychopath. The result is that Herod sets out to annihilate any threat to himself, and the family is warned in a dream to escape to Egypt.

After Herod's death, they eventually return to Nazareth, where Joseph sets up in the carpentry and general building trade.

Next time we glimpse Jesus, it's by the side of the Jordan as he asks his cousin John to baptise him. Now John is there to straighten out the people and Jesus is the one person who doesn't need that. John tells him so but Jesus insists. As he comes back out of the water, a voice from heaven declares: 'You are my Son. I love you and I'm so pleased to be your Father.'

Much of what Matthew tells us, you'll find in Mark – calling the disciples, healing the sick, telling the people what living with God means. But Matthew also records things you won't find anywhere else, including about the prophets. The Jews had been looking for centuries for the promised one. Most of them wanted an army commander to drive the Romans back across the seas. Matthew points out that what the prophets promise is not what the people have actually been praying for. Look again and see a Prince of Peace.

Mountainside teaching

The headline grabber in this gospel is the big message festival in Galilee. A crowd gathers round Jesus on the hillside and he begins.

If you feel you understand hardly anything about God, be reassured because heaven is designed for you. If you've lost the ones you loved, be comforted: God will fold his arms around you. And if you make space for others, God will make space for you.

Focus on what God wants – you'll be filled with deep satisfaction; show mercy and he will be merciful to you. If your heart goes out to others, you'll glimpse God himself; if you work well together, you're family; if you suffer because of your faith, heaven belongs to you. Be content in all these situations, tough though they may be. Whatever people say or do, hold on to your hope because heaven is a treasure and it's for you.

You are the salt of the earth, the people who preserve the best, the hands that heal the wounds, the ones who give others a taste of God's goodness, the lights that shine.

Think also about what God truly longs for and not whether you're ticking rule boxes. You've heard 'Do not murder', but anger can be bad, too. Don't turn up to worship while holding on to issues about other people. Make your peace, settle your disputes, then come. You know about adultery being wrong, but watch where those eyes linger. Just because your desires stay hidden doesn't put you in the right. Own up to whatever stands in the way of goodness and get rid of it. Remember that marriage is precious, not just a contract to tear up.

Don't use big words to make your promises sound more impressive. Say 'yes' or 'no'… and mean it. Don't try to get your own back, even if you've got a good reason. Let it go. Do more than people ask of you. Don't just love your friends – anyone can do that. Love the unlovely. Be a friend to an enemy.

The Lord's Prayer

Remember this too: God has absolutely no time for those who want to look holy and overwhelm him with meaningless words. Give quietly and privately. Pray because you need to and not because you want to be seen doing it. Like this.

Our Father, heaven's keeper,
you inspire awe and wonder.
May what you want actually happen here.
Give us what we need for today.
Be forgiving to us as we keep forgiving others.
Don't let anything impossibly difficult overtake us
and keep us safe from evil.
Amen

Don't make a show of doing something for God. If you do, you've already got your reward – people's sympathy and admiration. Instead, set about your tasks without any fuss. Don't hoard more and more stuff in this world. It doesn't last. Invest instead in the things that don't fade or grow tired. Whatever you treasure will be where your heart lives.

Don't worry or panic about what you need. God looks after his creation perfectly well. The birds in the sky are beautiful; the wild flowers look fabulous even when they only last for a day. Do you think God will lavish less care on you?

Stop fretting: it doesn't help you live a day longer. It doesn't put food on your plate or clothes on your back. Your heavenly Father knows what you need. He'll see to it. Give up adding the fears of tomorrow to the troubles of today.

What God loves… and hates

You need to find kind words. If you're harsh or dismissive about others, what do you expect from God? Your faults are probably greater than theirs. Keep asking, you'll receive; keep seeking, you'll find; keep knocking, the door will open. Why? Because God loves to give you good things. The heart of life in a sentence is this: do for others what you would want them to do for you.

It can be hard to live that way and easy to make different choices, but they lead to trouble. Look carefully at the effect people have: if they create trouble, they *are* trouble, even if the words they say seem perfectly respectable. Build your own life on firm foundations by hearing what I have to say.

The crowd in Galilee are stunned. This man talks as if he knows it for certain. And his words are matched by actions: healing a man with an awful skin disease, curing a Roman soldier's servant, even calming a storm.

Tough being different

There's no doubt that what's happening makes Jesus look like the one that the Old Testament prophets had promised. But, for some, his claims are too much. He not only heals people, but he also tells them their sins are forgiven. That's God's job in the view of his critics – too much authority for anyone on earth.

Some lives are changed, like a certain tax officer called Matthew, but others remain unconvinced. There are those who didn't like how his cousin, John the Baptist, lived and now they don't like this very different approach from Jesus.

It's not that Jesus demands too much: 'Come to me if you are weighed down by life and I will give you rest,' he tells them. 'Work with me and learn the rhythms of my spirit. Life will fit better and feel lighter.'

This is a new world where there's no limit for second chances, no end to love. But there are troubling things within his different way of thinking. 'Should I forgive someone as many as seven times?' asks Peter. 'Multiply that by 70,' says Jesus. A story about two people with debts explains the point: whatever other people owe you, it's nothing compared to what you owe God. Always and everywhere, mercy needs to come first.

What Jesus is offering is like hidden treasure that's worth giving up everything else for. But the fact that this is for everyone doesn't always make it easy for some. In one story, a master hires workers on a standard daily rate, which is reasonable enough. Later in the day, he hires more and, in fact, some are hired just for the last hour. The master pays everyone a full day's rate so those who worked from the start begin to grumble about unfairness. People are not always so keen on generosity when it's for others rather than them.

As the final clash with the authorities draws closer, Jesus tells the story of a father asking his two sons to do some work. The older one says: 'What? Me? You must be joking.' Later, he thinks about what he said and turns up to help. The younger one says: 'Certainly, father, it will be my pleasure.' But he does nothing about it. So, who did what the father asked? The religious leaders know it's the older boy, but they also realise the younger one represents them: the people who say the right words but don't act on them.

No turning back

The arrival of Jesus in Jerusalem for the coming Passover festival is met with great delight by his followers and the stories turn to how ready we are to face God. Jesus tells the tale of a wedding running late and of the girls who stay ready for the grand arrival versus those who have simply dropped off to sleep.

After that, there's the parable about the servants and their master's money. How you use what you are given is the challenge in that tale. The final story Jesus tells is about the last day of all. What divides people is not what they say but what they do. It's not about great saints or terrible rogues but about whether you do what you can, when you can.

Jesus has already made enemies in Jerusalem among the Pharisees because he's pointed out how their rules are closing doors to ordinary people rather than opening them. As a result, he stays safely out of the way at night in Bethany. It doesn't stop a plot to kill him being hatched and he's arrested late on Thursday at evening prayers after a final supper with his followers.

Peter has told Jesus that he'll stand with him to the very end. When it comes to it, he's ready for a fight but not to be arrested with Jesus, so he runs away. Later in the night, he denies even knowing the man he's followed so faithfully. Finally, he breaks down and weeps as he realises what he's done.

Jesus' trial isn't exactly legal but all that matters to the religious leaders is the guilty verdict. How it's been achieved doesn't bother them. And Matthew adds a particular sadness. Judas, who has sold the information about where to arrest Jesus, is struck by the enormity of what he's done. He's horrified and tries to turn back the clock by returning the money. Nobody wants it. In spite of all he's heard about forgiveness, the shadows are too great and he hangs himself.

Jesus has been heavily flogged by the Roman soldiers and is too weak to carry his own cross, so a passer-by called Simon is forced to do that. The nails are hammered in, the cross is lifted up and Jesus hangs there as his clothes are divided up by the soldiers. The ownership of his cloak is decided by a dice game while passers-by shout abuse. Amid all this, Jesus cries out: 'My God, my God, why have you forsaken me?'

As he dies, the earth is shaken and so is one of the Roman soldiers, who feels frighteningly certain that they have actually crucified the Son of God. The body is laid in a garden tomb provided by Joseph of Arimathea. There's a guard set upon it so there can be no grave robbing. The Jewish and Roman authorities agree on one thing at least: the dead need to stay dead.

The next chapter

That makes the events in Joseph's garden on the morning after the sabbath such an issue for everyone. Mary Magdalene and the other Mary go to the tomb, but the earth is shaken once more and the stone rolled away. Instead of meeting a guard, they're met by an angel whose appearance reminds them both of lightning and the whitest snow. 'Don't be afraid,' he says. 'He is not here, he is risen. Go quickly and tell the others that Jesus will meet them in Galilee.' Both terrified and joyful, they take the angel's message.

Meeting the risen Christ amazes and energises the disciples, but it creates a problem for the government. When the guards report to the chief priests what has happened, an appropriate strategy is devised. The guards are given a large sum of money to say that the body was 'stolen' while they were asleep, with a promise they won't get into trouble for this.

The story does its job in some quarters but not among Jesus' followers. Not only do they get to meet him again, but they're also given a new role. Jesus tells them: 'You're the next chapter. What I did, you'll do. Not just here, everywhere; not just now but till the end of the age. And who will be with you to make it happen? I will.'

The heart of Matthew

Written with a Jewish audience in mind, Matthew draws on material also found in Mark but links it to the Old Testament. There's a big section about the teaching Jesus did in Galilee, including his description of what makes you happy. Matthew has a deep sense of the power and authority with which Jesus spoke, plus an understanding of how this rattled people and eventually led to his death. It's clear how much it matters to know that Jesus is the Messiah: the one who was promised and is here at last.

Mark:
lots to do, must dash

Early records suggest that Mark was written in Rome when Nero, the emperor, started throwing Christians to the lions. What had been seen and heard about Jesus needed to be written down. This gospel takes us closest in time to the life of Jesus himself. In that sense, this is where it all begins.

The good news starts in the desert with a voice like thunder, getting the world ready. John is baptising people, straightening up their lives because someone is coming who will turn them inside out. When John baptises Jesus, it's clear who that someone is. The Spirit comes like a dove to rest on Jesus and a voice declares: 'You are my Son. I love you and I'm so pleased to be your Father.'

Forty days in the desert help Jesus to get sorted for the work ahead and the temptations which will come with it. Then it begins. He calls his first followers, heals the sick and talks about God in ways people haven't heard before. The message spreads like wildfire. So fast, in fact, that Jesus is soon forced to hide out in quiet places just to have a chance to pray. With all this busyness, not everyone is convinced he'll have time for them. A man with leprosy asks to be healed, 'if you are willing'.

'Of course I'm willing,' Jesus tells him. And the miracle happens. Now, the healings hit the spot, but the messages get mixed reactions. A man who appears through the roof of a house needs forgiveness as well as the ability to walk. Jesus gives him both, but the religious bosses hate it. 'Who does he think he is?' they complain, 'God?'

So much, so soon

You can understand the religious bureaucrats not liking Jesus. He creates a team of fishermen and tax inspectors instead of politicians and insiders; he socialises with the wrong sort, is easy-going about regulation and frankly doesn't seem anywhere near as serious as John the Baptist.

So they start looking for a way to catch him out. Jesus challenges them about their narrow-mindedness and, after he heals a man on the sabbath, they want him out of the way. He's beginning to look like a threat to their whole way of managing God.

For the moment, though, there are crowds so large so that Jesus nearly gets overwhelmed by them and escapes the crush by fishing boat. The inner team expands to twelve close followers – not to make them feel important but so they can share the work. The celebrity-style fuss results in Jesus' family trying to get him safely back home. For them, too much attention is not good news.

However, he's definitely not about to slip away quietly. There are stories to tell, like the one about a farmer who always gets mixed results with his seeds. That's what it's like with people and God, Jesus explains to the twelve. Many grow up to become something, while others… well, they go their own way. But remember: you *can* be the small light that brightens a dark place.

Miracles versus message

The words are paralleled by actions. In the middle of a stormy night on the lake, Jesus calms the waves. Later, he heals a man who seems to be drowning in an army of dark spirits. Next, he cures a woman, even as he makes his way to help a synagogue leader's daughter. So much is happening so fast that Jesus asks for the miracles to be kept quiet. His work isn't about grabbing headlines but capturing hearts.

The reaction to Jesus is mixed, especially in his hometown. You see, they remember him as Mary's boy, the builder. Time passes, teaching continues and the twelve close followers go out to spread the message.

Talk gets back to King Herod, who has beheaded John the Baptist. The gossip is that Jesus is John returned from the dead. The reality is even stranger. This is someone who heals the sick and feeds 5,000 by blessing a few loaves and fishes; someone who walks on water and who calms the wind and waves of a storm. Even his closest followers don't quite grasp what is happening.

Now, while the disciples don't get it, the Pharisees don't like it. They are the strict and exact element of the faith which maintains the old standards at all costs. Jesus tells them that their priorities are wrong. The minor stuff, that makes them look good, they do. The heart of the faith – helping each other – they avoid. In effect, they're cancelling out the very word of God that they say they're protecting.

The same is true about their food regulations. Instead of being ultra-particular about what goes into your mouth, Jesus tells his disciples to care instead about the words that come out of your mouth. That reveals who you truly are.

Even when Jesus wants nothing more than a quiet break, he ends up working: healing a Greek woman's daughter, then helping a man to hear and to speak. He wants this all kept low key, but people love to talk. The result is headlines for his miracles but much less understanding for his message. As his popularity spreads, he's also gathering enemies among the religious leaders, so happy endings for this story are starting to look less and less likely.

The one

The second half of the book deals with the long journey to Jerusalem. Up north, out of the way, Jesus has been teaching his closest followers. Eventually he asks the most critical question: 'Who do you think I am?' Peter goes for it: 'You're the one we've been waiting for, the Messiah.'

At last, Jesus feels he can speak about the hard times to come. But when he talks of his suffering and death, they aren't ready and Peter's response sounds more like the devil than the angels. Nobody likes hearing about pain, but sometimes that's what you've got to face. What good would it be if you saved your life and lost the one thing that made you truly human, your soul?

On a mountainside, Peter, James and John see Jesus utterly changed. His clothes become dazzling white and they see the prophets of old, Elijah and Moses, speaking with him. A voice rings out telling the three disciples to listen to Jesus.

Then they are alone with him again and, like so many strange and wonderful moments, it's followed by a problem. The other disciples have failed to cure a boy of his fits and there's an argument about who is to blame.

'Please help him, if you can,' says the boy's father.

'If?' says Jesus. 'Everything is possible where people have faith.'

The father's reply is simple. 'I do have faith,' he says, 'but I need your help with my doubts.' The boy is healed and Jesus reminds the disciples just how much they need to keep praying.

Not all about you

On the road again, the disciples are soon squabbling among themselves about who will be the greatest. Jesus tells them that a good leader doesn't seek power and privilege. If you want to be first, be last; if you want to lead, be there to help everyone.

There's teaching on not thinking you've got exclusive rights to God's work, a reminder of the sanctity of marriage and a welcome for children. If people are to find where God is, he tells his followers, they need to trust like a young child would. There's also a sombre warning not to make the way difficult for others by what you do. Stay friends – it matters.

A rich young man discovers how money can get in the way of following Jesus and the road to heaven suddenly seems hard, so Jesus has to remind his team that it's God who makes things possible, not us.

While Jesus is reminding the disciples of the suffering and death to come, his close followers are still debating which of them is most important. The idea of serving each other simply isn't sinking in.

The final stop before arriving in Jerusalem for the Passover festival is Jericho. It's where Jesus heals a noisy, blind beggar called Bartimaeus, who joins the group as they head for a big entrance in Jerusalem. Jesus rides in on a young donkey and the crowds come out shouting that he's the one they've been waiting for. When he gets inside the city, he takes a look around and returns to the suburb of Bethany for the night.

Crooks' corner

The real action starts the next morning when Jesus takes on the temple traders, the people making a rotten profit in the house of God. He tells them: this is a place for prayer, not a corner for crooks.

That's what causes people to plot his death: the challenge to those with comfortable seats in places of power. It doesn't happen immediately. He's too popular for that. But the plan to get rid of him begins to take shape.

Although some leaders try to catch him out, it's not all disputes. One teacher asks him what matters most. 'That you love God with all your heart, soul, mind and strength,' he replies, 'and love others as you love yourself.'

Jesus doesn't think like most people. When a widow puts two tiny coins into the offering box, he can see it matters more than the bigger donations. For her, it's all she has.

While he recognises goodness when he sees it, Jesus talks as well about troubles to come and the future destruction of the temple itself. His own trouble is much closer – the teachers and priests are already wondering how to arrest him secretly. One of his own disciples, Judas Iscariot, provides the solution: for a modest fee he will find a good moment to hand Jesus over to them.

Before that, there is a moment of extravagant love. A woman pours expensive perfume on Jesus. Some think it's a misuse of money, but the kindness touches Jesus and he tells them she did a beautiful thing that helps prepare his body for his burial. His time is drawing near and he knows it.

Under cover of night

Each evening, Jesus stays safely out of the city, but on Thursday he slips back secretly to Mark's house to celebrate the Passover supper in Jerusalem itself. It's a dark time. He knows that someone close will betray him. 'My body is given for you,' he tells his disciples, 'and my blood seals God's promise to you.'

After the meal, Peter promises Jesus that he'll stand by him whatever happens. Jesus warns him it may be harder than he thinks and they all walk to a quiet garden called Gethsemane for evening prayers. Jesus is distressed as he prays about the suffering he knows he will face, but his own disciples are too exhausted even to stay awake and support him. Judas leads a crowd armed with swords and clubs to the spot. A signal for the arrest has been arranged. It's the traditional welcome kiss. And that's how Judas betrays his master.

Everyone runs except Jesus and a young man, who escapes after some of the men make a grab for him. They only get hold of his clothing and he runs away naked. It's a detail that makes little sense unless Mark was actually there.

A trial is cobbled together and the religious leaders use what Jesus says about being the Messiah as proof that he is guilty of blasphemy. He is blindfolded, beaten and sent to Pilate, the Roman governor. Meanwhile, Peter has slipped back into the city to follow his master, only to panic when he gets close and is challenged by a servant girl who is sure that he is one of the team around Jesus.

Peter denies it – three times. Then he hears a cock crow and he remembers how Jesus warned him about all this. The man who prided himself on his bravery is devastated by the speed with which fear overwhelms him. He breaks down and weeps.

The Place of the Skull

Pilate's first morning job is to deal with a gaggle of Jewish leaders baying for someone's blood and the calm dignity of the man in question. He's puzzled by the accusation that Jesus is the king of the Jews and gives the prisoner a chance to defend himself. Astonishingly, he doesn't.

As a gesture of goodwill at this festival time, it was the custom to release a prisoner. So, Pilate offers to release Jesus or a murderer named Barabbas. He knows that the leaders have only handed Jesus over to him out of jealousy. But the chief priests stir up the crowd to shout for Barabbas, the convicted killer.

To satisfy the crowds still shouting for Jesus to be crucified, and even though the crime isn't clear, Pilate has him flogged and sent for execution. The soldiers increase the agony. They mock him, strip him of his clothes and dress him in a purple robe as if he's a pantomime king. A crown of thorns is quickly hooked together and rammed on to his head. Then they spit on him and beat him.

Jesus is led out to death, already so battered that he cannot carry the cross beam for the crucifixion. A passer-by called Simon from Cyrene is forced to do it. When they reach the Place of the Skull, Jesus is nailed to the cross.

His reward for being a healer and teacher like no other is to be scorned and mocked in an agonising death. A sign on the cross says: 'The King of the Jews.' To many around, he becomes their cheap entertainment. They yell for him to save himself if he's the Messiah. No wonder he feels forsaken and lost as he hangs there, but he sees it through to the end. And the way he dies shakes the soldier in charge to the core. For him, at least, Jesus truly is the Son of God.

The death of Jesus is witnessed too by the women who had faithfully followed him.

Then, a surprise: a Jewish leader takes a deep breath and decides to stop being a secret supporter. Joseph from Arimathea cannot bear to see the great healer's dead body left out to be ripped to shreds by dogs and vultures, so he requests permission for burial from Pilate. The body is placed in a linen cloth and the tomb entrance is sealed with a massive stone. Mary, mother of James, and Mary Magdalene watch the work taking place.

Not finished after all

It looks done and dusted, except there's one further twist. The next day is the sabbath, a work-free 24 hours, but on the morning after that, several of the women return to the tomb to complete burial duties. What they find is the massive stone rolled away, no body and a young man in white. They are terrified and bewildered, even more so when he says that Jesus is risen and they must tell the disciples to meet him in Galilee.

And that's where it stops, even more abruptly than it began… in the middle of a sentence. No one can be sure why and maybe somewhere there's a missing part of this gospel that kicked off with the promise that the good news starts here.

The heart of Mark

Mark – written to get information down at speed with dubious grammar and plenty of people namechecked. A first half of stories, healings and arguments with the authorities. Then it's the road to the Place of the Skull, with a focus on Jesus' last week. No elegant introductions, no neat ending and not written to impress anyone with its style but to tell you as simply as possible how it was.

Luke:
outsiders on the inside

Luke appears to be the only writer in the New Testament not from a Jewish background. The gospel was researched and put together for someone in Rome called Theophilus, probably a senior government official. It's the one which makes clear from the very beginning exactly why it's being written: to investigate and organise the best eye-witness accounts about Jesus.

Luke opens the story with an old priest named Zechariah. His life mixes hope and disappointment. He should be a grandfather by now, but he's not even a dad. Then, an angel pays a visit: 'Your wife Elizabeth will have a son, a special child, a voice to prepare new ways as Elijah did.'

'We're old,' the priest replies.

'And I'm Gabriel,' says the angel.

Zechariah is struck dumb by what has happened, even more so when a baby is indeed on the way.

Strange kind of blessing

Next stop for Gabriel is Mary, Elizabeth's cousin. She's about to be married to Joseph. Great news, explains the angel, you're going to have a child, Jesus, who will be called the Son of God. Mary is understandably shaken by this and wants to know how it will happen. The answer is that the Holy Spirit will come upon her. It's not the most everyday answer, but Mary says, if it's what God wants, it's what she wants.

The next months include time with her cousin, Elizabeth, and a poem – the Magnificat – that's has Mary's smile shot right through it:

God took one look at me – someone who was no one –
and filled my soul with dancing joy.
From this day on, people will look at what God has done
and call me blessed.
The proud stumble, the rich lose out, leaders fall to earth,
but the poor and hungry find all they need.
God's promises are coming through;
the world has turned and mercy is the winner.

Mary returns home to Nazareth and Elizabeth gives birth to a boy who will become known as John the Baptist. Zechariah then finds his voice again and speaks of how John will prepare the way as God breaks through the dark shadows with salvation's dawn.

Birth in Bethlehem

In the meantime, it isn't looking all that bright for Mary. Heavily pregnant, she has to make the journey from Nazareth to Bethlehem for a census caused by the government's new tax demands.

The accommodation isn't great, as all the normal guest rooms are full. When Jesus is born, shepherds come to visit. They've been stunned and amazed by angels telling them of the Messiah and spread the word about him. It's a similar response from Simeon and Anna when Mary and Joseph take the baby to the temple. 'This is it,' Simeon sighs happily, 'this is the one it was promised that I'd see.'

Things are less straightforward in Jerusalem, twelve years later, when the family are back for the annual Passover celebration. They travel with a big party of pilgrims from Nazareth. On the return journey, Mary and Joseph think their lad is in the group and they've been walking all day before they discover he isn't with them.

When they get back to the city, Jesus is nowhere to be seen. Eventually, they find him in the temple discussing faith with the teachers. Everyone seems amazed at what he knows. Jesus appears surprised that his parents didn't realise where he'd be. Mary thinks deeply about what's happened and Jesus grows in every sense of the word: well-thought-of, not just by those around him, but by God too.

Changing times

The story of Luke then moves on almost two decades. It's year 15 for Emperor Tiberias, but the first year of John the Baptist's work telling the nation about someone who is coming to change and save the people. He's baptising as a sign that people are straightening out their lives.

That 'someone' who's coming turns out to be John's cousin, Jesus. He gets baptised, as everyone else does, then a heavenly voice is heard: 'You are my Son. I love you and I'm so pleased to be your Father.'

After time in the desert, struggling with the temptations his work may bring, Jesus takes his message to Galilee. It starts well, but in Nazareth he's rejected as just another local lad, Joseph's boy. Elsewhere, the word spreads: this man is amazing. He heals people, talks about God, gathers together a group of friends and followers. Change is not just in the air, it's happening.

Luke covers much of the ground that Matthew and Mark do: telling people where true happiness lies, saying how far love must go, learning not to judge others and finding ways to build on firm foundations. But Luke also has stories that are found nowhere else. At Nain, Jesus stops a funeral procession. A widow has lost her only son and is inconsolable. 'Don't cry,' he whispers, and, touching the coffin, he calls the young man back to life and to his mum. It's terrifying and exhilarating at the same time, and the news of this healer spreads like wildfire.

Wiping the slate clean

Jesus welcomes all sorts of people. Sometimes that creates tensions. He's having dinner with a pillar of the Jewish faith, called Simon, when a woman appears. Now, she's seen a good deal more of life than frankly she should have done. Bad news in most people's eyes.

With tears running down her cheeks, she washes Jesus' feet and then pours expensive perfume over them. Simon thinks: 'If this man was who he claims to be, he would have realised how wicked this woman is and would have stopped her.'

Jesus knows what's on his mind: 'Simon,' he says, 'two people owe money which they can't pay. One owes ten times as much as the other. Who will have more love for the person who writes off their debt?'

'The one who owed more,' he replies.

'Exactly! You forgot some of the welcoming things a host should do. She didn't. She remembered it all and did so much more.' Then he tells the woman that her sins are forgiven and that creates an even greater stir. Only God can forgive sins. Who on earth is he?

Everyone, evermore

Part of the answer to that is someone who has time for everyone. The twelve disciples travel with him, but so do many women, including Joanna, Mary Magdalene and Susanna, who provide practical back-up. And when a disciple wants to stop some other people's work because they aren't part of *our* group, Jesus will have none of it. 'Those who aren't against us are for us,' he tells his followers.

It's not just twelve disciples either. Seventy-two followers are sent out in pairs. The reason for it is clear: they need to use everyone they can to share the good news, heal the sick and make this world God's world.

Like Matthew and Mark, Luke includes Peter's realisation that Jesus really is the promised one, alongside warnings of his suffering and death. These are woven throughout the gospel alongside some of the best-known stories Jesus told which turn up only in Luke.

A Jewish leader who can recite the rules of the faith well enough tries out Jesus with a tricky question. Exactly who *is* my neighbour? Jesus tells the parable of the traveller who sets off alone down the Jerusalem-Jericho road, one of the most dangerous in the country. Bad decision! He's attacked and left for dead.

It looks like it's all over, but then a priest comes by. Lucky break? No – the priest is scared that it's a set-up to rob him too, so he gives the injured man a wide berth. A religious studies teacher does exactly the same.

Then a Samaritan comes along – different tribe, different version of God, different history – distinctly them, not us. He's exactly the person you don't want to see when you're in a mess. But he's the one who helps. His heart goes out to the man in trouble and he gets him to a safe place. What's more, he pays all the bills. Who's your neighbour? The person who behaves like one.

Later, at Martha and Mary's house, Jesus takes a well-deserved rest. Martha is getting things ready and her sister is just listening to the teacher. Martha is frantic with all the work she's doing. Eventually, she interrupts: 'I'm doing all the work and she's just sitting there. Tell her, Lord. Make her help.'

'Martha,' Jesus says with real warmth, 'you fret too much about so many things. Let it go. Learn to listen. That matters more than anything.'

This isn't an excuse to do nothing. If someone is ill, Jesus helps them, even on his day off, which seriously annoys those who believe that having a nice quiet religious day is more important than making people well.

Practical work needs to be matched by practical prayer, and Jesus offers a simple and short way to do this. He also reminds them of the need to persist with what you're doing. Not everything happens instantly.

Don't bank on it

With Jesus, the focus is on sharing rather than storing. There's the story of a man with a bumper harvest who built bigger barns to keeps his crops safe and secure for the years to come. Plan A was to sit back and take it easy. Of course, there was no Plan B. He got it all sorted… and promptly dropped dead. So the question is: where is your heart – with all your stuff or with all that God loves?

Luke highlights the message that you can't love both God and your bank account. Crooked managers, rich men behind closed doors and money-loving religious people all turn up on these pages to highlight the same contrast: either you're focused on yourself and fixing things to make your own life extra special or you're doing what you can to make other people's lives better.

It's hardly surprising that Jesus is not exactly popular with everyone and he recognises it. He knows he's asking people to take a way that isn't always easy and which means changes in the way you practise your religion. It costs.

From the bottom to the top

Things never work out quite as you expect with Jesus. The ones who are least in this world will suddenly be first; the ones who believe they deserve special treatment will be last.

The heart of the work is with people who know they need help. If a shepherd has lost one of his sheep, doesn't he go out looking for it? That's what God does for you, Jesus tells them. If someone who is lost can be found, it fills God's heart with joy.

Even when someone's gone off and spent every penny on big parties and bad people, God wants them home with him again. It may not please those who think God belongs exclusively to them or those who are sure they don't need help, but it pleases God.

The generosity of God is one of the great threads in Luke, but there is an equal focus on the need for those who live comfortably to help those who struggle to simply live. Not expecting to be thanked simply for doing what you're supposed to be doing also gets a mention. If you've got a job, get on with it.

Luke is full of encouragement not to lose heart. Think about this, Jesus tells his team. There's a widow with absolutely no influence in a town and there's a judge who is plain lazy – not even slightly interested in justice. The widow has a case but the judge ignores her. End of story? No. The widow keeps turning up, bothering him. Eventually, he gives in and sorts the case out because he can't take it anymore. She's worn him down, you see. Well, if you can get bad judges to listen simply by nagging, think how much more you'll be heard by God, who loves fairness, if only you don't give up on prayer.

Of course, it needs to be the right sort. Imagine two men praying, says Jesus. The first, when he prays, thinks of what he's achieved and is glad to have a chance to remind God about it. The second has always squeezed as much money as possible out of people, is ashamed of what he's done and asks for forgiveness. It's the one who knows he needs help who gets heard. If you think you're great, you're not; if you know you're down, you can be lifted.

The man with one last chance

As Jesus turns to go to Jerusalem for the final time, he makes a friend from among the men with big pockets and small morals. Zacchaeus, the tax collector, is too short to see the great teacher in the crowd so he climbs an overhanging tree to catch a glimpse of him.

Jesus spots the figure in the branches and invites himself to dinner. Not a popular decision, but a new chapter for Zacchaeus, who gives half his money to the poor and pays back anyone he's cheated. That's what Jesus is about: finding those who have lost their way, saving them from their selfishness.

When he enters Jerusalem, it's to the sound of cheering supporters who have been briefed that Jesus is coming and they treat him like a king. But the party atmosphere doesn't last. Jesus is troubled not only by the corruption he sees in the temple itself but by the sense that, one day, the city that he loves will be no more.

The tensions grow even as the people turn out to hear him teach in the temple. His criticism of the religious leaders means that they want to arrest him, but it looks too risky given his popularity. Instead, they pay people to ask apparently innocent questions that might undermine his reputation – fake sincerity for political gain.

Dead men don't eat fish

By the time of the Passover meal on Thursday, the authorities have a plan. Judas, one of the disciples, has been tempted to swap sides and has agreed to find a moment when they can arrest Jesus. This meal is the last one Jesus shares with his followers and it's something he has so wanted to do. But the atmosphere is overshadowed by what he knows is coming – the giving of his life for them.

The betrayal takes place after evening prayers, when soldiers arrest Jesus and politics take over. The disciples scatter and he's brought before the Jewish council. Outside the house where he's being held, Peter joins a small crowd around a fire. He's recognised as one who was with Jesus but denies he even knows the prisoner – just as Jesus had warned him he would. When he realises what he's done, he retreats and breaks down in tears.

Jesus is found guilty of claiming to be the one sent by God – blasphemy. He's sent by the Jewish council to Pilate, the Roman governor, who passes him on to King Herod. Herod is interested in the man but passes the decision back to the governor. Pilate can see no reason for execution, but a mob has been whipped up to shout for crucifixion.

They get what they want and the nails are hammered in. Even as this is happening, Jesus asks his Father to forgive them, for they don't know what they are doing. He hangs there alongside two criminals. One shouts abuse. But the other asks Christ to remember him when he comes back as king. Jesus promises that he'll be with him in paradise even before the day is over.

Death comes and, with it, darkness. Joseph from Arimathea provides a tomb for the burial. It's followed by a day of rest, a sabbath.

Then, early on Sunday morning, Mary Magdalene, Joanna and Mary the mother of James take spices they've prepared to the tomb in order to complete the burial duties. It never happens. The body has gone. It's a puzzle and there's more to come. Two men whose clothes seem to blaze with light tell them that Jesus is risen.

When the women try to repeat this to the disciples, the men think it's nonsense. Nonetheless, Peter goes to check. He's amazed, but not as stunned as the two followers Jesus meets on their way to the nearby village of Emmaus.

Bit by bit, the truth sinks in. Jesus is back, and he even eats a chunk of cooked fish with the disciples. A bit like putting up a sign that says: 'You *can* believe your own eyes – dead men don't eat fish.' Being sure of what they've seen matters because they are the witnesses. They will receive his power. The good news will now be theirs as much as his. As Jesus blesses them, he leaves and is taken up into heaven. But the end, for once in this life, is only the beginning.

The heart of Luke

Luke – a book that shares plenty of material with Mark but pays special attention to the troubled, unloved and plain unlikely. This account includes characters who many people might reckon are not good enough and parables that turn normal thinking upside down. It's the gospel for everyone, no matter how far they've wandered, no matter how confused they've become.

John:
the word is out

The first three accounts of Christ's life are called synoptic gospels – they see things in a generally similar way. John is different. There is more about who Jesus was rather than what he did, maybe because his readers already knew that. Clement of Alexandria, writing around AD200, saw it as a supplement to the others. About a century later, Eusebius records that the gospels of Mark and Luke were in circulation while John was still preaching. He notes that John was happy that they were reliable accounts but felt there was still more to say.

In the beginning, he was there:
the Word – the breath that begins everything.
Not a single thing was made
that didn't have his signature on it.
Then, suddenly, he was here, the light of this world.
Most people walked right past him.
But some saw what was happening
and, for them, life started all over again.

That's how John draws his listeners to him – with a kind of mystery story. Eventually, he reveals who he's been writing about: Jesus, called Christ, the Messiah announced by John the Baptist. When people meet Jesus, they're impressed, ask to follow him, then they bring their friends along. It's the start of what will become the twelve disciples and many other followers as well.

In next to no time, Jesus is turning water into wine at a wedding party. Everyone is stunned and those who are following get the message: this really is someone they can believe in.

You'd think that would be the beginning of the good times, but John turns next to incidents and arguments in the temple in Jerusalem. Good and bad news jostle with each other in this book. People believe in the miracles but their hearts aren't entirely won over. Jesus knows it and does not trust himself to them.

Unexpected meetings

However, at least one heart is changed. Nicodemus, a senior Pharisee, comes to him privately one night. That's a shock in itself. The Pharisees are the rule keepers, the ones who don't do different.

'You're from God,' he declares, but what he's saying trails off. Doubt hangs in the air. Jesus understands the depth of the change Nicodemus is facing. 'If you want to begin again,' he tells him, 'you need to be born again and feel God's Spirit at work.'

Month by month, the news about this new preacher spreads, and John the Baptist describes his effect as God's Spirit in full flow. The trouble is that success breeds enemies and Jesus returns to Galilee via Samaria. Now that's an area where the people aren't properly Jewish. They don't do things in the *right* way. When Jesus meets a woman at the well, he asks for a drink. She is shocked: 'From me? But you're Jewish. You can't stand people like us.'

That's the start of a conversation that astonishes the woman further still. Not only is he willing to speak to her, but he also tells her about living water – God's Spirit, with the power to transform the way she lives. And it's not just for one small group of people; it's for everyone. The conversation is so astonishing that she tells the whole village to come out and see him. After they've heard him as well, they agree. He really does seem to be the one they've been waiting for.

The problem with miracles

Next stop is Cana, where a government official meets Jesus. His son is seriously ill back in Capernaum. Jesus has become concerned that people only seem to believe if there are miracles (which they see happen!), but Jesus tells him that his son will live and he should go home. Instead of arguing, the official sets off and meets his servants, who have come to tell him that his son has started to get better. Sometimes, you simply need to take Jesus at his word.

The next miracle involves someone who can't walk home… or anywhere. He's been paralysed for 40 years and just sits by a pool which has alleged healing powers. Perhaps he still hopes; perhaps he's given up. The question Jesus asks him sounds too obvious: do you want to get well? The man doesn't answer the question.

Instead, he explains how it's only the first one in who gets healed when the waters move, and that's never him. Whether it's an excuse or the truth, we don't find out. Jesus simply tells him to get up and walk. And, to everyone's amazement, he does.

That convinces the Jewish authorities of the power Jesus has. It also shoots him up their list of dangers to be got rid of. On one level, the problem is that he heals people on the sabbath, when good people are supposed to be taking a rest. On a deeper level, it's about who is in charge. Old leaders don't like making way for new ones.

Delete fear, insert faith

What no one can deny is that remarkable things are happening. Jesus' disciples get caught in a storm on Lake Galilee and he walks across the water to them. They are terrified. 'Do not be afraid,' he tells them, a phrase he'll need to repeat time and time again.

On the hills above the lake, he feeds a crowd of thousands from two fish and five barley loaves. They love the picnic but don't really understand who he is. One day, the crowd wants to crown him as king and the next they're angry because he's talking about being the bread of life from heaven.

'Who on earth does he think he is?' they grumble. 'We know his parents – he's the carpenter's boy.'

Jesus is trying to explain how, as the promised one, he's come to fill their lives with what they truly need – a relationship with God. This isn't the political leader and all-conquering miracle worker many people have dreamed of, and they simply drift away.

'Do you want to go, too?' Jesus asks his close disciples.

'Lord,' says Peter, 'where would we go? The words that give eternal life come from you, nowhere else.'

Not what everyone wants

These are hard times. Jesus is hated, moves around secretly and even his own brothers aren't convinced. When he does preach in public, opinion is divided.

He continues to talk about lighting up the world and letting the truth set you free, but the religiously-rigid crew remain determined to miss the point. They think they're already home and dry with God. Jesus tells them that life is not about good connections but right actions.

In the midst of this, Jesus heals a man who was born blind. Plenty of people can't believe it's actually the person they once knew. They assume it must be his twin or someone who looks like him.

'No, it's me all right,' he tells them. The establishment decide they need to quash the story. However, the man at the centre of the storm sums up the situation for them: 'Once I was blind, now I can see.' He gets banned from the temple for his honesty.

The problem in a nutshell is this. Jesus is claiming to be the one who will save them and open the road back to God. He's the shepherd who will protect and give his life for them. For some, that's too big a claim. At the winter festival in Jerusalem, it comes to a head. People get ready to stone him and Jesus is forced to slip away quietly, back to the River Jordan area, where support for him remains strong.

Dead man walking

You might expect Jesus to stay where people truly believe he is the promised one about whom John the Baptist spoke, yet, suddenly, he's preparing to go back to Jerusalem. His disciples are flabbergasted: 'But they tried to stone you there!' The reason for the change is a message from Mary that her brother Lazarus is ill. By the time Jesus arrives, Lazarus is dead.

Mary's sister, Martha, still hopes desperately that something can be done. When Jesus weeps, people see how he loved his friend. But love is only the beginning, because he calls Lazarus to come out of the tomb where he has been laid, and they see a dead man walking. Suddenly life after death is not simply a discussion topic, and many who see what he's done believe.

An event like that doesn't take long to become front-page news. The religious bosses are more worried than ever. The Romans are not going to like this, they observe, and we'll feel the effects of their anger. Caiaphas, the high priest, is clear: it is better that one man dies before riot or rebellion puts at risk their hard-won rights under Roman law.

 They give orders that anyone who knows where Jesus is must tell them. It's not necessary. Jesus doesn't slip quietly into Jerusalem for the Passover; he turns up in a blaze of glory on a young colt with crowds cheering and yelling his name.

It feels like the promised one has arrived to take over where King David left off. The Pharisees think they're getting nowhere, but Jesus is already troubled by the days ahead. He knows how quietly and quickly day turns to night.

To my Father's house

At the Passover meal on the Thursday, Jesus ties a towel around his waist and washes his disciples' feet. Servants are supposed to do that and Peter is clearly shocked. But a servant is exactly what Jesus is. Status doesn't matter, caring does. He warns that one of them will betray him, but it just seems puzzling to them all.

'Love one another,' he tells them, 'as I love you. And don't let worry take over. I'm going ahead so that there'll be a place in my Father's house ready for you.'

The disciples don't really understand all this, but Jesus promises them his Spirit that will transform them and make sense of it all. They'll need to stay connected to him like fruit on the branches but, if they do, all that is good in them will come from him and they'll find a way through.

Yes, they'll face troubles, but they will know deep peace as well. There'll be much to learn, but everything will work out. He prays for them: that they may be kept safe and their hearts filled with joy. Then they make the journey to a quiet garden just across the Kidron Brook for evening prayers. They've been there many times before but this night, soldiers guided by Judas Iscariot, swoop to arrest him and the disciples scatter.

Blood

Later, while Jesus is being questioned by the authorities, Peter is back in the city warming himself by a fire and hiding his identity by denying he knows the prisoner. As the morning comes, there's the sound of a cockerel and he remembers what his master had said at supper: that before the cock crowed Peter would disown him three times. As for Jesus, he's shunted across from the Jewish authorities to the Roman governor, Pontius Pilate.

By this time, there's a crowd gathering who want blood. Pilate can't find a good reason to condemn Jesus but that's not enough to save him. He gives way and sends his prisoner to be whipped, then crucified.

Jesus is taken to the Place of the Skull and hangs there upon a cross while the women who loved him so much watch on, as soldiers gamble for his coat. Night starts to fall; the soldiers check the crosses and find that Jesus is dead. Just to make doubly sure, one of them stabs his side with a spear.

Breaking out

Then, the strangest twist of the story: two members of the Jewish council which condemned him – Nicodemus and Joseph from Arimathea – decide to break ranks with the establishment. Joseph asks Pilate for permission to bury the body decently and they place it safely in a tomb in Joseph's garden.

Thirty-six hours pass; Friday becomes Sunday. Mary Magdalene sets out to finish the burial rites. The sun is hardly up, the tomb is open and the body is missing. She runs to Peter with the news: 'They've taken his body and we don't know where it is.'

Peter and John set out to see what's happened. There's no sign of forced entry, just a neat set of grave-clothes. For the two disciples, hope dawns. But, for Mary, it still seems desperate. She stays in the garden, sobbing quietly.

'Why are you crying?' says an angelic voice.

'They've taken away my Lord and I don't know where they've put him.'

Then another voice, a man, asks her who she is looking for. Thinking that it's the gardener, she doesn't even look up: 'If you took him, tell me where he is and I'll get him.'

'Mary,' says the man and she thinks she recognises the voice.

'Teacher,' she says, and turns to be sure Jesus is really there. He is, and he gives her the role of being his messenger to the other followers.

No doubt about it

The disciples are astonished, but even more so when Jesus appears in the room where they've locked themselves away. Seeing their master just standing there saying, 'Shalom – peace be with you,' must have been hardly believable, so he shows them the wounds on his hands and side, then asks them to receive his Spirit.

The disciples are overjoyed. However, Thomas misses all this and so declares disbelievingly: 'Unless I can see and touch the scars myself, I'll not believe it.'

A week later, Jesus appears again and says the same thing: 'Shalom – peace be with you.' Then he turns to Thomas: 'Look at my hands,' he says, 'put your fingers there. And my side – put your hand there. No more doubt. Just believe.'

All that Thomas can say is: 'My Lord and my God!'

Jesus tells his disciples how remarkable it will be for those who don't get the chance that Thomas does and yet still believe. The faith and lives of future followers provide a great place to finish. But, after a tidy final sentence, something happens.

As with so many writers, there's an extra final bit. Much of it consists of a fishing story from Galilee. However, it's not the fish that matter but Peter's chance to get right with Jesus. He let his master down by denying he knew him… but he still loves him. Jesus gives him the chance to say it out loud.

A second chance is always a good place to end and this time John really does come to a close. But not before suggesting there are so many stories to tell that the whole world wouldn't have enough room for them all.

The heart of John

Written for a Greek audience fascinated by what lies behind all we see and touch, John gets his readers thinking hard about who Jesus is: light of the world, bread of life, good shepherd. Sometimes this reads like an eye-witness account and sometimes it's full of reflection, explanation and symbolism. It's like someone late in their life remembering what happened but also now understanding what it all means.

The Acts of the Apostles:
what, where, how?

The book of Acts picks up from where Luke's gospel finishes. Here, Luke observes the church as it takes its very first steps. It's about how God's Spirit inspired and directed that work, often taking it in unexpected directions. It's also the story of Paul, the great mission leader and defender of the faith, who could not possibly have imagined how his life would be turned around.

After Jesus: what, where and how? That's what the book of Acts sets out to describe. The followers learn it's their turn now, but Jesus promises that his Spirit will be there to work through them. Then, he's swept up and away before their eyes. They gawp – naturally enough – but are told not to just keep standing there. So it's back to Jerusalem to pray, think and be patient.

Wind and fire

At festival time, they discover what Jesus told them to wait for. And it's massive: like a wind that reaches inside and sets you on fire. Not so that you just feel nice and sit there smiling, but heart-burstingly good so that you want to go out and tell everyone. The crowd are stunned at what they see – preaching at breakfast time has never sounded like this.

The cynics put it down to drink but Peter says, 'Come on, it's only nine o'clock. This is bigger than wine. This is what the prophets went on about: seeing visions, dreaming dreams, being saved.' So he tells Jesus' story for the first time. 'It's for you and your children,' he tells them. 'Turn away from the bad things in your life, be baptised, know you are forgiven and feel God's Spirit.' Three thousand respond. Not bad for a first sermon.

Times of amazement

This is the honeymoon period for the new followers. They get on well with each other, share what they've got and are amazed by the wonder of it all. Not a surprise, then, that there are miracles, including a lame man healed by the Beautiful Gate. The religious bosses are nervous. Peter is preaching about a man they executed.

An overnight stay in jail and a grilling in front of the council for Peter and John is a warning not to keep speaking about Jesus. The authorities can't do much more because the crowd have seen the miraculous healing and are praising God for it. On their release, Peter and John meet with other believers to pray. Suddenly, the Spirit is shaking the building and everyone in it.

The feeling is fantastic – the new believers are like a single heartbeat, sharing all they have. But not everything's perfect. One couple offer to share some cash, then keep some back while pretending not to. Not a crime, but it's a dishonest way to treat the Spirit they've been given and the shock of being found out results in death. A dark moment in a time of miracles and wonders.

Healings continue, crowds of people become believers and jealousy among the Jewish leaders reaches new heights. The apostles are arrested, the prison doors are locked for the night and they're still locked in the morning. So it's a bit of a shock when the officials find them out preaching in the temple again. The leaders don't buy the story about angels setting them free, and they like it even less when Peter tells them that he needs to obey God rather than anyone else.

The Jewish council wants these troublemakers dead, but Gamaliel asks: 'What are you worried about? If it's yet another movement, it'll soon die down. They always do. But, if it's from God, nothing you do can possibly stop it. Leave them alone.'

With a whipping and a threat – the council's idea of what leaving people alone means – they are released.

Backlash

As the number of followers grows, there are tensions between some groups within the new movement and leaders are appointed to help. One of them stands out, Stephen – a great speaker, a miracle worker and wise, too. Even his enemies see something special in him.

Called before the Jewish council, he offers them a history lesson and a vision of Jesus in heaven. It's too much. In their fury, they stone him. As he's dying, he calls on God to forgive his killers. A bright young theologian holds the coats for the lynch mob. He's called Saul.

Stephen's death is the trigger for the backlash. Jerusalem becomes a dangerous place for followers of Jesus, with Saul as the leading hit man. People flee the city but they don't stop preaching. The Jewish council has unwittingly unleashed the first missionary teams.

When the crowds in Samaria hear God's word and people are healed, they are thrilled and many are filled with the Spirit. Amazing – the detested, not-quite-proper Jews are now part of the family. Then Phillip gets prompted to take the Gaza road where he meets a homeward-bound Ethiopian, and their time together results in his baptism, which in turn starts the church in Africa.

The risk

Meanwhile, Saul is doing what he does best: picking on the followers of Jesus. On the way to Damascus in order to find and imprison even more of them, it all changes. A blinding light, a voice – God tells Saul to stop persecuting him and to go to the city where he'll be told what to do. It looks like one of the most improbable turning points in history, but the effect will be spectacular.

Next, God calls Ananias and asks him to cure Saul of his temporary blindness. Ananias knows all about Saul and is probably thinking: 'If he sees again, he'll kill me.' But he does what God asks and nothing is ever the same again: Saul moves from being the one who imprisons the followers of Jesus to the one who tells Jesus' story so well that it astonishes those who hear him.

The change doesn't solve problems overnight. Saul has to be smuggled out of Damascus because enemies of his new message want to kill him. And the church in Jerusalem is terrified when he arrives. Frankly, they don't believe the story that he's now following Jesus.

Only Barnabas understands that belief in Jesus needs to be followed by belief in people too. In time, the support of Barnabas for Saul gets him accepted. Saul's preaching, however, puts his life at risk once more and he's sent to Caesarea and Tarsus. So the church spreads and grows.

Growing pains

The focus then shifts to Peter, who is preaching and healing wherever he goes. Along the way, he has a dream which shows him that the message is for everyone. Then he meets a Roman soldier called Cornelius, and God's Spirit comes to all who are hearing the word, whether or not they are Jewish. That's the moment when a radical group within the Jewish faith starts its transformation into a worldwide movement that includes people from all nations. In Jerusalem, there are doubts about this, until Peter explains what has happened to him and they begin to realise that God's message is for everyone.

In Antioch, the good news reaches the Greek community as well as the Jewish one, and Barnabas is dispatched from Jerusalem to help out. Later on, Saul joins him. It's here that the word 'Christian' first gets used: a name that seems to have stuck.

Back in Jerusalem, King Herod takes centre stage. Not a nice man. He has James, the brother of John, executed and, when that's a vote-winner, he grabs Peter. Sixteen soldiers are put on round-the-clock security, but he's miraculously set free. Herod executes the guards instead.

Peter can't quite believe in his escape and thinks it's a dream. A prayer meeting for him is even more astonished when he turns up. Praying is one thing, but getting answers like that is utterly astonishing to them.

Meanwhile, the church keeps growing. Saul and Barnabas go to Cyprus, with John Mark as their helper, to share God's word and to challenge those who are against it. The result is amazement followed by belief. And it's here that Saul begins to be known as Paul.

At Antioch, John Mark turns back to Jerusalem and Paul preaches so effectively that Jewish leaders, who don't want to see any change, stir up trouble. The result is that Paul and Barnabas get chucked out of the whole region for their pains.

Of course, each time those who hate change get Paul and Barnabas moved on, they spread the changes a bit further. After a promising start in Iconium, they get moved on again, but Lystra welcomes them like gods because they heal someone.

Paul has to explain: 'We're men like you: nothing great. It's God who's special.'

Once again, enemies of the new faith turn the crowd against them. This time, they stone Paul and drag him outside the city, thinking he's dead. But the disciples gather around him and he gets up. The next day Paul and Barnabas move on to Derbe, where many also believe God's message.

Making the break

Eventually it's back to Jerusalem, returning through the places they visited on the way out. Paul and Barnabas encourage people and appoint trusted leaders. On arrival in Jerusalem, they report to the church on what God's done and how the message is for everyone.

This leads to the big debate about whether Jewish regulations should apply to all new believers. 'Circumcision hasn't exactly turned us into a nation of saints,' observes Peter. 'And look at what's happening: God isn't making distinctions between people. Why on earth should we?' James, the brother of Jesus, agrees, so the big break is made. This is not going to be a revised version of the Jewish faith; God is going global, just as the prophets had promised.

Not everyone agrees about everything. Paul and Barnabas fall out about whether John Mark is reliable enough to travel with them. But the result is good – two missionary teams on the road instead of one: Barnabas and Mark to Cyprus, Paul and Silas to Syria and Cilicia, where Timothy joins them in the town of Lystra. It's a reminder to pessimists everywhere that not every problem has to finish up as a large-scale disaster.

For Paul and Silas, the next stop is Philippi in Europe, where Lydia, a successful businesswoman, is one of the very first followers and her house becomes the centre for the fledgling church. This is where Paul drives out a girl's evil spirit, gets jailed for his kindness, survives an earthquake, saves a prison guard from suicide and sings midnight hymns – all in 24 hours.

As God calls Paul to places like Thessalonica, Berea and Corinth, the usual pattern is a warm response to the message from some, with others stirring up jealousy and disputes. The Jews don't seem to like anything different and the Greeks find the idea of one God a bit limiting. But, everywhere, Jesus' story changes lives.

In Ephesus, Paul decides that he doesn't need to teach within the Jewish community if he isn't welcome there. And Christians realise that it's not enough just to sign up, you also have to get rid of the black magic stuff that you've stashed away in case of emergency. There are ups and downs, big and little issues, but, in Miletus, his message has the dark edge of goodbyes. Wherever Paul now travels, people gather with him and they pray together, sensing it's the last time they will see the man who has meant so much to them.

Into the frying pan

Paul is going back to Jerusalem. He knows there's trouble ahead and some try to stop him, but Paul says he's ready to die if needed for his faith. When he reaches the city, there's a warm welcome from the church and they work through the issue of Jews and other people sharing the same faith. A week later, it's a very different story in the temple as Paul is accused of betraying the Jewish religion and there's a near-riot. Roman soldiers grab him for his own safety.

The commander tries to sort out the issue the next day and fails. Paul is taken back to the fort where, that night, he has a dream. 'Don't be afraid,' Jesus tells him. 'You've told my story in Jerusalem; now it's time to go to Rome.'

Paul's nephew overhears a group plotting his murder, so the Romans transfer him under cover of darkness to Caesarea, where the governor is Felix. The Jewish authorities use a smooth-talking and dishonest lawyer called Tertullus to make their case. Paul simply offers the facts.

Felix reserves judgement because he *says* he's waiting for his commander to turn up from Jerusalem. The governor delays for two whole years, fascinated by this man who has been placed in his custody. Sometimes he's rattled by what Paul says, but he always comes back to hear more. It's as if the message is too fascinating to ignore and too frightening to accept.

One final journey

Felix is replaced by Festus, the case is reviewed and Paul appeals to Caesar. Before he travels, he has the chance to tell his story to King Agrippa, who agrees that he's done absolutely nothing criminal. However, he's appealed to Caesar so he's sent to Rome.

They sail first to Fair Havens, arriving on the edge of the stormy season. Paul warns against going further, but the experts think they know better. Mistake! A gentle wind soon becomes a hurricane and even the most hardened sailors think it's all over.

But Paul has a dream from God and tells them that everyone will make it to shore. Hard to believe in the circumstances but, on the 14th night, they run into shallow waters. The sailors try to save their own skins by planning to slip away in the lifeboat. Paul sees what's going on and tells the centurion, who cuts the lifeboat's ropes. If it's going to be drowning, they'll all do it together.

In the midst of this, Paul says: 'Time for a bite to eat. Keep your strength up and all that.' He may have sounded like their mother, but he turns out to be right. The ship runs aground and breaks into pieces but everyone scrambles ashore.

It's Malta, out of season and a bit rainy. The locals are kind and helpful. It turns into a winter where friendships are made and healings happen.

They make it to Rome the next spring, where Paul is allowed to rent a house. He can't travel now, but others can come to him so the story he's been given to tell continues. Some are convinced by what he says, some aren't; the Jewish leaders still disagree, even amongst themselves.

As for Paul, he goes on telling it like it is, which is exactly what he set out to do. As a last page, it's hardly a finish at all, but perhaps that's exactly right. Paul may have been at the heart of God's message in those early years, but what matters is that there's always someone to pass the message on.

Pointers for life in Acts

- Go where God calls you, even if it's not exactly where you want to go.
- Take care how a church acts and avoid getting into deep water.
- Be aware that prayer requests have a tendency to create answers.
- Realise life with God sometimes involves visions, dreams and promptings.
- Be practical – that includes a bite to eat in order to keep your strength up.

Romans:
thinking it through

This letter to the Christians in Rome was probably written when Paul was in Corinth. He hadn't met the church in Rome at this stage but was intending to visit them on his way to Spain. The city was at the heart of the empire. Its diverse people included Greeks, Syrians, Turks and North Africans. The letter isn't concerned with what Paul knows about the local church but rather what he knows about the faith. That's what makes it important.

A letter from Paul to the heart of the world in which he lives: part lecture, part passion, part puzzling over things like the rest of us, but starting, as he usually does, with a smile on his face.

How I thank God for what I hear about the way your faith shines out, he tells his listeners. That's great, especially as we've got such a powerful message – God can save anyone, everyone. All that's gone wrong he puts right, from start to finish. That includes things that people often seem to put up with: ungratefulness, juicy gossip, not being straight with each other. This is a wholehearted new beginning.

Love gift-wrapped

There's no excuse for reckoning you're better than someone else. God's kindness and patience aren't based on whether people deserve it or not. Whatever religious background you have, you don't do all you should. But God gives you a new start through the faithfulness of Jesus to everyone. That's love: an astonishing, wonderful gift. It's nothing to brag about, it's something to celebrate.

From the start, it's been about faith. You don't read that Abraham did everything right, but that he trusted in what God promised. If you've turned up for work, you get paid at the end of the month and you probably think: 'Well, I've earned that!' Things are different with God. We simply don't do this job of living well enough to deserve anything. If we walk his road, we do it together in faith – like Abraham.

Whatever's wrong needs to be put right and that's what Jesus does. When we were helpless, he became our help. Astounding! Sometimes people can put their life on the line for a good friend. That's hard. How much more remarkable that Christ put his life on the line for all of us. What he did makes it possible for us to have peace and hope with God.

Going beyond the rules

Paul reminds his readers about what happens in the Jewish scriptures. From Adam and Eve at the very beginning, the relationship with God was fractured. What Jesus did turned the world around. We are forgiven, put right with God, given new life.

So, should we go on sinning because there's so much forgiveness around? Absolutely not! We've been through the dark times and we're with Christ now – from here to eternity.

All the same, we still do wrong – and I'm no different, admits Paul. The law shows us where boundaries are, but I still end up not doing what I actually want to. My brain goes in one direction and my body heads off in another.

It's this mess that Jesus saves me from, Paul says. I could never manage that on my own, however hard I try, but God's Spirit holds me close. We're not simply part of the workforce; we're part of God's forgiven and forgiving family.

Nothing can divide us

Life's a bit like being in a tunnel: although you can't see the way ahead, you can be patient, trusting that you'll come out into sunshine. God's Spirit is with us, taking us through the dark times to the brightness beyond.

If God is for us, who can be against us? If he gave his only Son, how could he not give us all we need? And who can condemn us when he chooses to forgive us? So what shall separate us from Christ's love? Trouble? Pain? Poverty? Danger? No. We will make it through with strength to spare because Jesus loves us.

Neither life, nor death; neither angels of light, nor creatures of darkness; neither today, nor tomorrow – nothing in all creation can separate us from God's love that we know in Jesus.

The difficult part

That would make a tidy end to a great letter, but real life is complicated. Paul has problems to face about his own Jewish brothers and sisters. If God chose them, how come so many of them were against Jesus and his teachings? Why do they trust in rules and good work to put them right with God instead of embracing his loving arms? And what will happen to them?

Don't blame God, he tells his readers. He doesn't change his mind; he'll always keep his promises. Paul's heartfelt prayer is for his Jewish brothers and sisters to turn to Jesus. Just because there are new ones in the family doesn't mean the old ones are rejected.

This is the house where mercy lives and everyone can experience it. Paul doesn't pretend to know the mind of God, but he does trust in his love.

He also knows the big challenge is to belong totally to God. Never stop praying; never give up. Be hopeful, cheerful and work well together; be sensitive to how others are and honest about yourself. Do what you can, when you can, even for your enemies. Let go of revenge and bring down evil by being good.

Making people stronger

Don't try to excuse yourself from what the government demands of you, don't do things that could cause trouble for others, don't keep on criticising people. Instead, be open to those who don't see things quite like you do. Make sure your opinions don't mess up anyone else's faith. Love others just as you love yourselves – you owe that to God.

And remember: God does the judging; you do the befriending. We're here to make people stronger and better together. Accept one another just as Jesus has accepted you. And may God's Spirit fill you to the brim with joy and peace so that your hope just goes on growing.

Paul draws to an end by saying he's confident of their goodness and hoping they don't mind his strong reminders. He also tells them where he's going next and warns them against people who stir up arguments. Then he closes by declaring that the big secret is out. It's Jesus: the good news and our strength to stand firm, whatever comes.

A glimpse back at Romans

Your faith shines with the new start you've been given. Celebrate it, but don't boast about it. We're the ones whose actions never quite match our intentions. It's Jesus who puts things right by giving his life for us. Nothing can separate us from God's love, for we dwell in a house where mercy lives. Never stop praying; never give up; never write anyone off. Remember: God looks after justice; you look after each other.

1 Corinthians:
a better way

Setting up a church takes time and effort. In Corinth, Paul spends 18 months working as a tentmaker and preacher. Although many believe and are baptised, some threaten Paul with legal action for challenging their way of worship. The action fails and Paul stays some time before moving on. Later, he gets news that the church is swallowed up in disputes and drunkenness. All this as some go hungry. So Paul writes to them about what's happening and follows it up with a call to unity and love.

Every time I think about you, says Paul, I'm thankful for the love that God has blessed you with. He is never going to give up on you. So why are you taking sides and breaking into little groups? You can't replace what Christ did with faith in church leaders, whoever they may be.

I didn't go in for smart debating, Paul tells them. I wanted it to be God's Spirit who convinced you, not my own learning. The wisdom of human beings only goes so far. Some may think Christ's death on a cross was foolishness, but it's what sets us free and puts us in a right relationship with God. What God plans for those who love him is more than eyes have ever seen or ears have ever heard, beyond anything we can imagine.

Everyone is a small building block that helps to create this place where God lives. Work together in different roles in God's service, building with care. Focus together on Christ rather than comparing and competing with each other. Eternity is yours because of Christ. There's no excuse for being smug about what you do or opinionated about what's right or wrong with other people's lives.

What we are like

Paul admits that being a church leader can feel like being on public display but totally ignored. He started the church they belong to and fears they now think they can do what they like.

Face up to what's gone wrong, he demands, and put it right. Sort your problems out face to face, even if it loses you money. Freedom in Christ doesn't mean doing exactly what you like.

You wrote and asked me some questions so here are my answers. Being single is good; being married is good; sex within marriage is good. Accept what you are and where you are. Don't get unrealistically spiritual. Appreciate each other's gifts. Don't get distracted from God and don't make life difficult for those whose faith isn't as strong as yours. Then Paul defends himself from unpleasant gossip that suggests he's in it for the money. I haven't taken a penny off you, he reminds them. My reward was telling you about Jesus.

Failure isn't the only option

He also asks his readers to think about the amazing experiences the Israelites had as they left Egypt. The people of God should have learned something from that. Instead, they got involved in all kinds of bad stuff, tried to live off God's goodness and then grumbled about life. Don't follow their example and don't become too sure of yourself. Failure happens all too easily. But it isn't the only option – God always offers a route out of temptation.

Paul then turns to matters of worship in Corinth, including what to wear and how to conduct themselves. In this time and place, Paul is asking them to show respect and work in partnership. There is no place for cliques or thoughtlessness. Church is somewhere to give everyone their place and everyone some space.

Stay together in Christ. Let his Spirit inspire you to all sorts of helpful action, but not so that we become like clones of each other. We are different people with different ways and different strengths. It's like your body: lots of parts for lots of purposes, each of them useful.

Love to love

Knowing the value of each other creates togetherness, but what matters most is love. And, unexpectedly, these thoughts are wrapped into a beautiful poem.

If angels seem to speak through me,
If my faith has power to move the mountains,
if I give away every single thing I own
and I do not have love,
I am nothing.

Love is patient and is kind.
It doesn't want what others have got,
it doesn't walk around as if it the world belonged to it.
Love is not full of its own importance, is never rude,
is not looking out for number one.
It is not easily angered
and never holds on to grudges.

Love hates evil but delights in truth.
It bears all things, believes all things,
hopes all things, endures all things.
And love never fails.
Everything else is temporary.
Even the words God has placed on our lips
will pass away one day.
Then only three things will remain: faith, hope and love.
But the greatest of these is love.

The one who came back for us

Poetry is followed by down-to-earth detail, including the need to be sensibly organised and understood. The heart of the message is Christ: he died for all that was wrong in our lives but then returned. He came back for us, brings life to us and destroys death for us. Stand firm and keep focused on Jesus because nothing you do for him is ever useless.

Finally there are practical arrangements, Paul's personal signature and his love goes to all of them in Christ.

The message of 1 Corinthians

You're not part of a little group that thinks exactly like you do; you're part of a wonderful and varied family that only works well when it works together. Instead of being smug or opinionated or grumpy, we turn towards love, filled with truth and kindness. Let go of the grudges and self-importance. Arguments won't last for ever but love will.

2 Corinthians:
make room in your hearts

This is a deeply personal letter. Paul wants to re-establish a good relationship with the church in Corinth. Since his initial time there, he has visited briefly and has written several times, including at least one very sharp letter. He worries about their reaction to that, but Titus brings him news that it's had a good effect even if some problems remain. Paul opens this letter by explaining what's happened to him.

I haven't been across to see you recently because things have been tough, so bad in fact that we thought we might die. Thanks for your prayers. They helped. And God pulled us through. Actually, if I had visited, it wouldn't have made anyone happy. So I put my concerns into that letter you received, not to make you miserable but to make you realise how I care about you and want you to stand firm in the faith.

Your happiness matters to me. If I made you sad, who would be left to cheer me up? Now I know you've been dealing with the one who started all the trouble. Yes, there has to be punishment but no, it's not the end of the line. We need forgiveness, too, or evil gets the upper hand.

Breeze-blown beauty

When you tell people about Jesus, it's a lovely thing, like the sweet smell of flowers on the breeze. This isn't just about good advice but eternal life through God's Spirit. It's like a curtain being drawn back so the sunshine floods in.

Talk about Jesus should be straightforward, open, honest and clear. God himself gives us this opportunity, so let's not get discouraged. He brings light to the heart of darkness and that's what makes us glow.

Yet this great shaft of hope is housed in fragile human beings, who are no stronger than everyday clay pots. We hit all kinds of trouble but we don't walk away; we're unsure of what to do but we keep looking; we're knocked down but we get back up again. Our bodies carry the aches and pains of this life and they sense death just like Jesus did. But we also carry the life that comes from him both now and for ever.

We have good reason not to lose heart. Even though it might look on the surface as if we are falling apart, inwardly we are being renewed day by day. That's what we focus on because it will last forever.

Crazy for you

We want you to have reasons to be proud of who we are and how we live, rather than what we look like. If people think we're crazy, we're crazy for God. If people think we're sensible, it's because we want to make sense for you. Anyone whose heart is joined with Jesus is different. It's like creation starting over again, sweeping away the past and making enemies into friends.

It's a twisted world, where we can be called liars for telling the truth, but we've tried hard not to create difficulties and we've never closed our hearts to you. In my eyes, you're still family. We've hurt no one, exploited no one. Make room in your hearts for us.

Titus has told us how sorry you are for what's happened, how ready you've been to defend me. That puts a great big smile back on my face. If getting problems out into the open has led to a change of heart and faithful living, there can be no regrets in that.

Confident or big-headed?

Paul writes next about practical help for the Jerusalem church and then the tone suddenly switches. Some people have thought this must be part of another letter. Then again, it's possible that, just as Titus brought a better report about Corinth, so another messenger arrived with less good news.

Some people seem to have moved from confidence in Christ to sheer big-headedness about their leadership. If you want to boast, declares Paul, boast about Jesus. Nothing else. If so-called super apostles are setting themselves up, remember that service to God is about humility and the message of Christ. Stick with that. Don't be led astray.

Paul then reminds them of his credentials as an apostle. He points out that he never took a penny for his work, that he's been beaten, imprisoned and shipwrecked in the course of his ministry. In fact, he still suffers in all kinds of ways. It's an impressive but odd kind of CV. As he says, if I'm boasting, it's about the things that show Christ's strength working through my weakness as I serve him.

I want to visit you again, he tells them, and it's not because I need your cash or want to be a burden but because I care about you. Will you love me less because I love you so much?

To be frank, I'm afraid I'll find gossip, quarrelling, bad tempers and worse when I arrive. Take a hard look in the mirror and be honest about what you see. I don't want to find you in a mess. I long to build things up, not tear them down. Make that possible for me.

Try your best in whatever you do, find good ways to solve your arguments, live in peace and may the grace of the Lord Jesus Christ, the love of God and the fellowship of the Holy Spirit be with you... all of you.

The message of 2 Corinthians

If we feel fragile, it doesn't mean we're not useful. Even when our bones ache, our hearts are still beating. We may seem crazy, but we're crazy for the right reasons. The most beautiful message has been given to us to share, so don't let quarrels or big-headedness cast a shadow across the sunshine of God's love.

Galatians:
old rules and new lives

Galatia is part of modern-day Turkey. It's a region rather than a city, so Paul may well have intended this letter to be read in several churches. He'd visited the area more than once and people were kind to him. But something has gone seriously wrong. Like many of Paul's letters, the reason for writing is to put that right.

Paul starts this letter by reminding people they can trust him: he's a senior leader, not because a committee voted for him or a friend got him the job, but because Jesus called him. That's important because he opens up with all systems firing: I'm shocked, stunned, amazed – I can't believe how fast you've dropped the good news for an alternative version. Except, of course, there is no such thing. Just because people seem pleasant or even very religious doesn't mean that what they say is right.

Going back

It's not obvious at first what Paul is on about, but the mist soon clears. The Christians in Galatia have been visited by a group who claim it's not enough to have faith and follow Jesus. They must also follow what Moses said, including about men being circumcised. It's not the physical operation that bothers Paul, painful though that may be; it's the idea you need to obey Jewish laws to be a follower of Christ.

Locking people into the old ways simply won't work, he declares, and I should know because I followed all of that better than anyone. Rules don't save you. Jesus does. Full stop! He puts us right with God. There's nothing we can do that adds to that.

This isn't my message, Paul tells them, it's the one God gave and it was approved in Jerusalem by James, Peter and John. Later on, in Antioch, he recalls how Peter was pressured into following Jewish regulations again and how he himself challenged this. It's not following the rules that gives you a relationship with God; it is Christ's love, and it is forgiveness.

Tick-box trouble

The basic question is simple. When you first sensed God both around you and within you, was it because you ticked all the boxes of the Jewish law or did you hear the good news about Jesus and respond with your heart? And, if this all began with that Spirit of God rushing through you, do you want to finish this life huffing and puffing in your own strength? Abraham stuck by faith. Why can't you?

The law showed people what's right and wrong, but people couldn't keep to it – not all the time. So we became trapped. That's what Jesus frees us from – all of us – whatever race or religion. In Christ, we become one family. Following the law of Moses in all its religious detail is not what's important. The only thing that counts is faithfulness expressed through love.

This, of course, isn't an excuse for doing whatever you want. Drunkenness, immorality and jealousy just show the evil part of human nature taking over. So does getting one over on others in the name of ambition.

Instead of all that, use Christ's freedom to allow his Spirit to flower. Care for each other, especially through the hard times, never becoming weary of doing good things. Be gentle with those who fail – we all have weaknesses and no one should be left to cope alone.

Inside out

The final words are written in Paul's own rather large scrawl because he wants it to be clear it's from him. Some people, he reminds them, still focus on the law of Moses and how things were. But one thing matters: Christ. His death on the cross creates a new world and makes us new people.

How we are on the outside doesn't matter, Paul explains. It's how we are on the inside that counts.

Galatians in a glimpse

Keep all the good things going. Be gentle with those who fail. Faith means following Jesus, not imprisoning yourself in the past. The Spirit of Christ isn't given so we can tick a set of boxes but so that freedom may flower.

Home
Exile
Love
Faith
Home

Home
Exile
Love
Faith
Home

Home
Exile
Love
Faith
Home

Home
Exile
Love
Faith
Home

Ephesians:
the heart of the message

If you go to Ephesus today, you'll only find ruins. Back in Paul's time, it was different. The city was the beating heart of the shopping world. There was also a stadium, a theatre, a harbour, a gymnasium and a temple, which was one of the Seven Wonders of the Ancient World. This isn't one of Paul's letters filled with people's names and particular incidents, so it's probably not intended just for Christians in Ephesus itself but for all the churches in the area.

Part of the family from the dawn of time, full to the brim with every blessing you could imagine, saved from the consequences of the mess you make, through the life and death of Jesus. That's the wonder of what God's done for you, and that's how Paul's letter to the Ephesians starts.

It's like a massive notice that says:

- you're welcome
- you're included
- you're forgiven.

So it's no surprise that Paul's prayers are full of thanks. But there are wishes as well. I want you to be wise, he says. I long for the eyes of your heart to be opened wide to all the people who have followed Christ across the years and the blessings that are ahead.

Whoever you are

The big message is that the people who follow Jesus are one team. This isn't about sections or styles; it's about being together. Whatever your background, wherever you come from, you are built into one church by Christ and powered by the same strength that raised him from the dead.

Looking back, Jesus brought you into the life you have now because of his love and forgiveness. You can't buy this or earn this. It's God's gift, full stop.

You were once outsiders in God's world, but now you're right in the heart of the family. That's what Christ's death did: it abolished distinctions, broke down barriers. The real secret of Jesus is that there are no secrets: everything of God is given to everyone on earth. That's what I give thanks for, time and time again.

I pray too that love may be the starting point for all you do, as you begin to understand just how amazingly wide and strong Christ's love is. I say these things in the presence of the one who has the power to do so much more than we can ever ask or imagine.

One in everything

Go where God calls you, do what he asks of you. Don't be full of yourself but be gentle, patient and tolerant with each other. There is one Spirit, one body, one Lord, one faith, one baptism, one Father God.

Jesus didn't come to earth to give you something special so you could start creating differences and divisions. It's time to grow up. Don't get pushed about by every religious fashion. No one has ever said you have to look like each other or do exactly the same thing, but you do need to be able to work together.

Don't let your desires control you or tell lies or let anger get a grip. Don't become bitter or hold on to that urge to get your own back. Be honest, kind, forgiving, and do a good day's work! In short: live in the light of God's love.

Making lives better

Grasp the simple truth that you're not here to be in charge. Your roles are about making things better, just as Christ's life was about serving others. This goes for wives, husbands, parents, children, slaves, masters. Play your parts, play them well and, whatever you do, don't make other people's lives more difficult.

Being a Christian means getting equipped. It isn't always going to be easy. Evil has a thousand faces and a million tricks. So let truth and faith and salvation be more than words; make them your armour-plated protection. Add that to a life where you act fairly and you'll still be standing at the end of everything.

Drench your life in prayer, not just thinking about yourself but also about each other and all God's people. Finally, pray for me in prison, that I won't become afraid of speaking out.

Tychicus will bring you all the news with this letter. He'll give you confidence and cheer you up. I'm sure of that. Peace, love and faith be with each one of you as you keep on loving Jesus. No exceptions, no end!

Ephesians: an invitation card

Welcome to a different team – one in which you're included, forgiven and saved from the consequences of the bad things you should have walked away from. Drench your new life in prayer, let faith protect you and play your part. You're no longer an outsider; welcome to the heart of the family.

Philippians:
a thank you in troubled times

Philippi was a bustling Greek city on the main east-west highway and home to the first church in Europe. It was also where Paul ran into trouble on his travels for undermining a fortune-telling business. He was flogged, stuck in jail for a night and told to move on somewhere else. You might expect a grumpy letter after all that, but what you get is a bit of a surprise.

This is a thank-you to the generous Christians who live in Philippi. They've cared for Paul and helped him out, which cheers him up no end. The Philippians are not just on his mind; they're in his heart and he wants their love to go on growing.

Paul is writing from prison, so others have taken on the preaching. Some are doing it out of love. Others just relish the opportunity to show what they can do. It doesn't matter, he tells them. If the message of Christ goes forward, that's good enough.

For his own part, Paul simply hopes he can do what he's called to do and be brave, even if he's sentenced to death, because he knows Christ will always be there. So he's not afraid of death, but being alive might frankly be more useful at the present moment.

Make my joy complete

Of course, it's not just about what Paul can do. Everyone has a part, he says. If Christ's nearness to you has brought you any encouragement, if his love has brought you any comfort, if his Spirit has taught you any tenderness, make my joy complete by being a team. Don't put your own career in the top spot. Let other people be number one in your world.

Don't muscle your way to the front of the queue. Think like Jesus. He took the bad with the good and, worst of all, was crucified for something he hadn't done. But then God lifted him higher than everything else put together. His name has become the best of all names, the starting point for the biggest festival of joy in the universe.

You did the right things when I was with you, he explains, so go on doing them now that I'm elsewhere. Discover just how wonderful it is for God's love to work through you. Don't grumble, don't argue, stay straight with God and shine like stars on a dark night. I want to feel that what I told you wasn't wasted. If I lose my life here, I'm going to go home joyfully. You stay happy, too.

Caring and sharing

I hope I can send Timothy to visit because he's worked alongside me like a son. Lots of people are wrapped up in their own little worlds, but Timothy has the good news deep in his heart. I know he cares for you.

In the meantime, Epaphroditus is coming over. I think you heard he was sick and he became worried that you were worried! Well, 'sick' hardly describes what happened: he very nearly died. So give him a massive welcome as someone who risked his life for me and for Christ's work.

Stay close to God. We used to put our trust in things that *we* could do. Don't. Instead, trust in Christ. You wanted things done to the letter of the Jewish law? I was your man. All that reliance on tradition is behind me: like rubbish, swept away. If I feel right today, it is not because I followed the rules; it's because of my faith in Jesus. All I want to know is him, as I share in his sufferings and get to know the power of his resurrection.

Keep on running

It's like the runner who keeps going to the end of the race – you forget what's behind and concentrate on what's ahead. Many get distracted by the world around and it eats away at them. We're focused on the transformation that Jesus brings.

I love you and long to see you. You bring me joy and make me proud. So keep the faith, stay strong, be gentle. Don't worry, be thankful, ask God if you need help. And may his peace, which is beyond all our understanding, keep your hearts and minds safe in Jesus.

Finally, whatever is good, whatever is true, whatever is fair and innocent and lovely, whatever is appropriate to say and do in God's presence, think about those things. But don't just think about them. Put what you have learned into practice.

Thank you for caring about me. I've learned to be content whatever happens, but the money you sent was a big help. It made me feel that I was not alone. Just as you've seen to my needs, may God look after you and may his love be with you as much as it is with us.

Philippians: heartwarming highlights

Make my joy complete by playing your parts together. Ditch the grumbles; avoid the arguments; light up the night with the goodness of your lives. Whatever are the kindest and best things you can possibly imagine: think about them and let your love keep growing.

Colossians:
complicated isn't clever

Paul is under house arrest in Rome. Timothy is there to assist him, as is Epaphras who helped to start the church in Colossae. Paul has never been there, but is so concerned at what he hears that he writes to them. The letter is also to be read in Laodicea. It's delivered by Tychicus and Onesimus and sets out to put the record straight about the faith.

A letter that starts with the positives: thank you, says Paul, for your faith and your love. It helps to keep the good news moving forward. May you grow wise; may you stay strong; may you be joyful. That's what God brings as he rescues us from the darkness of our lives without him.

This is followed with a poem of celebration:

Can't see God? Not sure what he's like?
Look at Christ.
Everything in heaven and earth,
everything seen and unseen.
Every good thing comes through him.

He was there from the beginning, holding the world together;
he's here now, head of the church;
he's gone before, the first to pass through death to the life beyond it.
No one else is like that;
he's number one, full stop.

It was good in God's eyes
to be totally there in Christ
and, through the sacrifice made on the cross,
everything in heaven and on earth comes back together.

Food and fuss

Paul is reminding people of where their strength comes from: they can stand in God's presence because of Jesus. It's about what he did, not what they do. That's how Christians in Colossae had started out. But there are some groups who love to add rules which make simple things look difficult, and no one has the courage to say complicated isn't clever.

He tells the church to focus on Jesus instead of rules about what to eat or drink. The worry is that some people become more concerned about sounding good or looking holy than they are about being part of the team.

The real wonder is that Christ lives in you, explains Paul. That's the key to unlock the puzzles of this planet, not senseless argument. God put you right, forgave all your sins and you don't need anything on top of that.

The message to those who want to add in extra rules or ideas is simple: stop it. Don't let other people tell you what to eat and drink; don't listen to those who say, 'Oh… I wouldn't touch that.' They may seem clever, more God-centred or even incredibly humble. They're not. Ignore them – they've lost sight of where we're going.

The first ingredient

Set your heart on how Jesus would act; see things from his perspective. You're a new person now and Christ is all that matters. God loves you and chose you to be his special people. Get rid of the bad stuff like greed, anger and insults. Keep your mind and tongue pure. Put up with each other.

Show forgiveness – after all, you need it yourself. Be gentle, kind, humble, patient. Most of all, show love to each other because it's the one ingredient that makes everything else work.

Paul reminds them to live in peace. They each have a role: wives, husbands, children, parents, slaves, masters. Do what you need to do as if it's for Jesus – because it is.

Work together

There's a balancing act here: rights and responsibilities. In the time when Paul lived, this is ground-breaking stuff. Everyone has a place and everyone is as important as everyone else. No wonder Paul was unpopular with the people who wanted the best seats in the house and the unquestioning obedience of others.

Keep on praying, he says, and remember us when you do, as we try to keep sharing the good news about Christ. Be wise as well in what you say about Jesus. Be pleasant, be interesting, use the time well and choose your words carefully. Bring out the best in those you meet and answer the questions you are actually asked.

Don't forget me here in prison, Paul asks as he signs off, and may God be kind to you. A simple and personal finish to a letter dealing with at least some church people who don't seem to do 'simple' at all.

The challenge in Colossians

Grow wise, stay strong and be grateful. Look at Christ and you're seeing the sheer wonder of creation. Watch and you'll see what forgiveness does, how it knots back together all that is bruised and broken in us. When Christ has done that much, don't complicate life by adding extra rules or by trying to be extra holy. Be gentle, kind, patient and play your part… just as Jesus did.

1 Thessalonians:
in the right direction

Paul visited Thessalonica after leaving Philippi. He was there less than a month because he caused a riot. Not that it was his fault. Some of the Jewish community didn't like what he said so they stirred up a mob to get him driven out. As soon as he can, he sends Timothy to find out how the new church is doing. Not bad at all, is the answer. But a little bit of support and advice looks sensible.

Grace and peace, write Paul, Silas and Timothy. We thank God that you turn faith into living and love into practical help. May that go on happening. Life hasn't been easy for you or us. In spite of that, you took the message to heart with the joy that God's Spirit gives. You really know how to welcome people – so much so that everyone else talks about it.

No sugar

Our visit had its problems, but it wasn't a failure. We told it as it is. You got the good news, straight. There was no flattery and no charge: the money we needed we worked for. Comfort and encouragement were the way we tried to get you started. Like us, you've suffered as followers of Jesus. But you're our hope, our joy, our very best reason to celebrate. We never forget you and long to see you again.

That's why we sent Timothy: to help you keep going. To be honest, I couldn't bear it any longer. I wanted to know you were okay. It's so good to hear I needn't have worried and that you care about us as much as we do about you. May the Lord let your love grow.

Make your relationships faithful – ones that would bring a smile to God's face. Live quietly, do a good job and mind your own business, not other people's. That way you can earn respect from everyone.

Fit for life

It's easy to be overwhelmed by sadness when someone you love passes away. Keep believing in Jesus. He died but rose again, so we'll be with him forever. People may worry about what this means, but you don't need to. As you live in faith, hope and love, you're right with God and you're ready.

Respect those who point you in the right direction, stir up the lazy ones and encourage those who don't think they're worth much. Help those who need it, be patient and at peace with each other.

Don't pay back bad with bad; turn it around and fill the world with good things. Seek joy, whatever the season. Stay prayerful, whatever the hour. Be thankful, whatever the situation. Let God breathe freely into our world. Don't get in the way of his Spirit but check the messages you hear. Throw out every kind of evil. Keep only what is good.

And may the God of peace make every bit and every part of you into the person he wants you to be. Pray for us, read this letter to others and may the love of Jesus be with each one of you.

Discovering Paul in 1 Thessalonians

- He's not a one-man band but part of a team.
- He tells it like it is – straightforwardly.
- He pays his way whenever he can.
- He knows not to worry about the detail but to trust God.
- He's concerned about how others are doing.

2 Thessalonians:
stay in the today

This letter is a follow-up and may have been written only shortly after the first one. Christians in Thessalonica are being persecuted. Paul writes to reassure them that they are not living in the final days of this planet and that God is with them.

Greetings from Paul, Silas and Timothy.

Thank you for being the kind of people we can tell others about: faithful, loving, caring… even in bad times. That's what it's all about.

Everything put right

I know you're all at sea right now, but God knows how you are persecuted for following Jesus and what a struggle it is. That doesn't mean the final days of this world have come yet but, when they do, everything will be put right as if in a single breath.

God's Spirit saved you as you heard the good news, found faith and became his people. Hold on to that; grip it tightly. Feel encouraged, strengthened and ever hopeful because of Jesus.

To be honest, admits Paul, our own lives are not always safe, so remember us in your prayers. And may Christ's power get you through life's troubles as you grow in him each passing day.

Work well

Work well and, as you do so, watch out for those among you who are lazy and disruptive – those who are not busy, but busybodies. Help them to settle down and earn the food they eat. It can be easy to let others take the strain. Everyone should be doing what they can. We worked when we were with you; we didn't cost you anything.

Do the things that make the world a better place. If someone is ignoring the message, there's no need to get into a fight about it. Simply say what needs to be said and leave it at that. But don't treat such a person as an enemy; they are still family. As you live in this way, may the Lord be with you and give you peace.

Yours, in my own handwriting, Paul.

Encouragement from 2 Thessalonians

- God knows how life can be a struggle.
- He sees how you care for each other.
- Where your power fails, Christ's strength still holds you.
- And, one day, all our troubles will be past.

1 Timothy:
sense, not nonsense

After Paul's letters to churches, the Bible collects together four of Paul's personal letters. This one is to Timothy, who is younger than Paul but works closely with him. His background is mixed: Jewish mother and Greek father. Paul knows the family. At this moment, Timothy is in Ephesus, which is clearly proving to be a challenge for him.

Someone has to stand up to those who like nothing better than a long and complicated argument. We're not here to win a debating trophy for the best speech about nothing much; we're trying to let love grow. The rules are there simply to make clear what's right or wrong, not to start a discussion group. This is Paul writing to Timothy in a letter that gives advice but most of all provides encouragement and support.

Hold on

Keep going, Paul tells him. Hold on to this: Christ came to save sinners. And look no further than me for an example of Jesus showing unlimited patience. I was the one above all others who persecuted his first followers. If I can be forgiven, anyone can. That's the miracle of mercy.

Prayer is at the heart of this life – not just praying for people you know but for everyone, including politicians and leaders. Salvation isn't just for some people but for all. It's easy to get angry and it's easy to obsess about how you look. That's what some people do in this world. Don't worry about having the loudest voice or being the one that others notice.

It's great that people want to be church leaders but you need to know what's required. No heavy drinking, money-grabbing or troublemaking. We're talking calm and collected here – well thought of, faithful in marriage, good at bringing up children, gentle, welcoming and experienced. People who take any position in church need to have proved themselves. No one should be going into it for what they can get out of it. And their assistants need to be as solid as a rock, too.

I hope to come and see you soon, but until then hold tight to Jesus, who came as one of us and showed us the power of God's Spirit.

Keep it simple

Of course, some reject this simple message. For them, morals are about what not to eat and why you shouldn't marry. It's false. Everything that God has created is good when it's in the right place.

Go on teaching. Work at it. Keep a close eye on what you say and do. Don't let anyone put you down because you're young. You've got gifts. Don't be impatient with those who are older and be an encouragement to others. Care for those who really need help, not simply those who claim they have problems.

Pay people what they're worth. Don't believe everything people say, but be ready to warn those who have done wrong… if you have the evidence. Don't expect to be aware of everything, whether good or bad: some behaviour is very visible, while other acts just stay hidden. Whether you're in charge or not, play your part with a real respect for others and for yourself.

Some argue that religion can make you rich. Ignore them. We brought nothing into this world and take nothing out of it, so be rich in contentment rather than cash. Keep well clear of this kind of argument and stay focused on eternity. Don't get distracted by smart talk. Be loving, reliable, gentle and faithful, and may God's blessing go with you.

1 Timothy: how to make a difference

- You don't succeed by arguing over the little things; you do it by letting love grow.

- You don't have to have the loudest voice; you'd be better with the strongest prayers.

- You don't need to be well-paid, but you do need to be faithful and keep it simple.

Home
Exile
Love
Faith
Home

Home
Exile
Love
Faith
Home

Home
Exile
Love
Faith
Home

Home
Exile
Love
Faith
Home

2 Timothy:
your turn now

This is Paul's final letter. Winter is coming; Paul senses his death is creeping nearer. He's imprisoned: not just under house arrest in Rome but in a dungeon in chains. Perhaps because of this, the second letter to Timothy is deeply personal.

Dear Timothy: like the son I never had. It's such a joy to see how you've turned out. Straightforward faith seems to run through your family: from Lois, your grandmother, to Eunice, your mother, to you. Keep that fire burning strong, remembering how, when I laid hands on you, God's Spirit of power and love lit up your life.

Our confidence is in how God loves us, how Jesus saves us. It would be easy to be ashamed of me being here in prison. It's just as easy to get embarrassed about sharing the good news. Please don't.

Be proud of my suffering for Jesus and accept that bad times may come your way too. Lots of people have deserted me, but Onesiphorus searched me out and stuck by my side, not the least bit embarrassed or scared that I'm in jail.

Not just you

Tell Jesus' story… but not all by yourself. Get reliable, honest people teaching alongside you. It may still be tough at times, but it's the same whatever you do: it's the hard-working farmer who gets the produce!

I'm in chains now but the message isn't. If we die with Christ, we'll live with him; if we don't give up, we'll be by his side through all eternity. If we turn our back on him, he'll turn away too, but if we simply fall behind, he will always wait for us.

Don't get drawn into nit-picking about details. The church, like everything else, is a real assortment. Become one of the best bits of that mixture. You need a clean heart if you're going to be useful to God, so avoid all the rubbish that goes on. Be someone God can use: kind, patient, faithful and easy to get along with. You'll meet indulgent, self-important people and those who take advantage of others. They may appear quite religious but it won't be real.

Stay true

Stay true to yourself and what you've known from childhood about Jesus who leads us to salvation. Read the scriptures – you'll find God breathing right through them. Those words are practical in all kinds of ways: equipping us to work well, showing us how things are, how we are and how we need to be.

Preach the message even when it isn't popular. But, if you're pointing out what's wrong, don't be a misery about it. Cheer folks up; be patient.

There will come a time when many will only hear what they want to hear and the silliest stories will be the popular ones. Stay calm; work hard; endure suffering if it comes your way.

I'm near the end now and, when I cross the finishing line, I trust that God will be there for me. These days only Luke is still with me. Try to come… and bring Mark too. He'd be a great help. And my coat – I need it. Oh… and my books so that I can keep studying.

At my first court hearing, no one stood by me – they just left me to it. May God forgive them. But the Lord gave me strength and what I said meant they didn't execute me there and then. Still, step by step, he's taking me to heaven. Please do your best to come before the winter closes in. God be with you; grace be with you.

2 Timothy: final instructions to a friend

- Stay true, for it's a joy to see who you've become.
- Work with a team you trust and don't get drowned in detail.
- Read the scriptures and sense the very breath of God.
- Be kind, patient, useful, cheerful.
- And may God's love be there in all you do.

Titus:
necessary, practical, useful

Titus is one of the people who became a follower of Jesus without having a Jewish background. He had travelled to Jerusalem with Paul and is now one of the team helping to establish the church in Crete. Today, the island is a great holiday getaway. Back then, it was known as a cheat's paradise, so what Titus was doing couldn't have been easy. That's why Paul wants to encourage him.

From Paul, a servant who works to light the way, to Titus who shares this work.

I've left you in Crete to choose the leaders there. We need good people, respected by those around them. If they're big-headed or enjoy an argument, they're not for us. If they like money or too many drinks, it won't work. We need those who welcome and encourage people, but who will also stand firm for what we believe.

It's a tough call on an island where even the locals complain about the laziness and dishonesty they see, and where one group teaches nonsense about Christians having to follow the old Jewish rules.

Sensible and merciful

Your teaching needs to be solid and sound, says Paul. Tell the older members to behave wisely and well so younger ones see how to live. And remember that Christians work hard for their bosses as well as for God. Faith does not give anyone the right to become awkward. Friendly? Yes. Gentle? Definitely. Peaceful? Absolutely. But not difficult.

Jesus didn't save us because of something brilliant we did but because his mind was fixed on mercy. The Spirit he brings us is so powerful, we can only describe it as starting life all over again with everything in the right place between us and God. This should mean people look out for each other rather than spending their time on useless details and endless quarrels. If some folk keep on causing arguments, warn them and give them a chance, but don't let them go on doing it.

Paul promises Titus that he will send Artemas or Tychicus to help, and invites Titus to take a winter break with him. He also asks him to help Zenas and Apollos start their own work. That kind of detail sums up what is at the heart of this letter: practical advice to help people lead useful lives.

Titus: what we're looking for

Troublemakers don't deserve publicity; faith doesn't give you the right to be awkward and, if you enjoy money, drinking or bossing people about, you're no help at all in this team. On the other hand, if you teach sensibly, encourage people and know how to be a friend, you'll be just what we need.

Philemon:
slave or brother?

Everyone has to ask for a favour now and then, even Paul. He's discovered that Onesimus, who is working with him, is actually a runaway slave from the household of Philemon, a senior member of the church in Colossae. Paul knows what he must do. Onesimus has to go back. But Paul doesn't want him walking into trouble, so this letter is a delicate business.

Dear Philemon and all my friends in the team at Colossae, I may be in prison for Jesus but it puts a smile in my prayers each time I remember you. People are in good hands when you're looking after them.

Can I ask you for something? I know I could insist, but love doesn't work like that. Here's what has happened. A young lad called Onesimus has been helping me while I am in chains. Yes, *your* Onesimus! The one whose name means 'useful' but who was so useless when he worked for you that I doubt if you've even missed him. He's useless no longer. In fact, he's been a terrific help.

Even so, I can't keep him here, much though I'd like to. I suppose I could see him as your gift to help me in prison but it wouldn't feel right if you weren't free to choose what to do. So I'm returning him to you.

Not as a slave

Perhaps the reason you lost him for a while was to find him forever: not as a slave anymore but as a brother. He matters so much to me but even more to you, and I know you'll value him both as a worker and as a Christian. If I'm your friend, welcome him back as you would welcome me.

If he owes you anything, I will pay you back. Here, let me write this in my own hand. 'I, Paul, promise to pay you.' Please, cheer me up by doing me this favour. I know you will. I'm sure of it. In fact, you'll undoubtedly do more than I ask. And one more thing: get a guest room ready. I have this great hope that God will answer your prayers for my freedom. Believe me, if he does, I'm coming!

Philemon: a postscript from history

Normally we wouldn't have any idea about what happened when this letter was delivered. But about 50 years later, Ignatius is writing a letter to the church in Ephesus in which he talks a lot about their much-loved bishop. He's called Onesimus. And Ignatius makes exactly the same joke about his name that Paul does. If this is the same person as the runaway slave, it would explain why the church had kept such a personal letter.

Hebrews:
keep the faith

Hebrews is described as a letter but reads more like a speech, a team-building call to a group of Jewish Christians. The writer urges people on to greater effort and fuller obedience. They need to keep going. Even when times are tough, there's the promise that God will be with them.

Back in the past God gave his message through the prophets, but today he's spoken in Jesus, who created and sustains the universe itself. Let's not go back to the darker days. We've been given a big step up into the sunshine, as the story streams direct from the creator of it all. At the heart is Christ, who lifts us into relationship with God: his death destroys death itself.

Road home

Our lives are a journey where we're always looking for somewhere to call home. Back when Moses led our people through the desert, that 'somewhere' was the promised land. Not everyone made it because they took their eyes off God and did things their own way.

Today, we're not travelling to a land across the river; we're heading for heaven itself. But we need the Spirit of Jesus lighting up our darkness and breathing through everything we do.

Stand firm in the faith and understand that Jesus is like a high priest: someone who can speak for us to God himself. He knows how being human hurts at times, how painful life can be, but he stayed close to God and did all that was asked of him. Even though he never failed, he knows how we feel and God makes him the one road onward for all of us.

On solid ground

We don't need to teach you again about the basics and how Christ has brought us into relationship with God. You've heard that and could be teachers yourself by now. Go forward and never be tempted to abandon what you have found. Actually, we're confident in you. You believed, you loved each other and you still share what you have. Keep that enthusiasm burning.

The letter reminds listeners about how, in the past, priests such as Melchizedek helped connect the people with God. Now the world has changed and we have the very best person of all to stand up and speak for us – Jesus.

In the past, things didn't work out because people couldn't keep their promises. Neither beautiful worship nor careful sacrifice can hide our faults; no one ever left the temple in Jerusalem with a perfect heart. That's why Jesus didn't give new rules for worship; he gave himself. In him, we have something that isn't going to crumble or fall short. What happened before was like a shadow. Now we have the real thing.

Never lost

It's Jesus who makes it possible to enter right into the very place where God lives. He gave up his life so that we might have clean hearts and find a door open for us. We can live for the first time as we were meant to live. Hold tight to the hope you have and look after each other. Don't give up on worshipping together or step back into old habits. Stick with Jesus.

You suffered and didn't give up; you stayed cheerful even when people took everything you had. Why? Because they couldn't steal the things that last forever. Don't be afraid. We are the people who don't turn back; we have been found and we will never be lost again.

Faith makes us sure of what we hope for but cannot yet see. It's always made the difference. Noah built his boat; Abraham went on his journey; Moses led the people out of Egypt. None of these followers could see where they would end up, but they trusted that God was leading them. Whether it's the Red Sea parting for God's people to cross or the walls of Jericho tumbling at the sound of trumpets, the heart of our history is faith, even if it sometimes led to suffering or death.

Running when it hurts

With so many heroes to cheer us on, it's like running the final leg of a relay. We just need to keep our eyes on Jesus at the finishing line and go for it. Sometimes that's painful, but it's nothing compared to what he suffered.

So, lift up your hands even if they feel like lead and keep on moving even when you think your legs can go no further. Be at peace with each other, too. We're going to a place where goodness and joy will be unshakeable.

Yesterday, today, forever

Look after those who need your help and keep a welcome ready. The next knock at the door might be an angel! Remember and care about those who are suffering or in prison as if it was you there. Love the one you're married to but don't love money.

And remember this – God never abandons us. Jesus is the same, yesterday, today and forever. Listen to those who lead you and don't get distracted by strange teachings. Pray for us, too, especially that I might be able to come and see you soon.

The letter closes with a blessing, greetings from Italy and a word about Timothy. These days it may seem hard to follow in places, but the encouragement is clear. We're on a journey but, with God, we never travel alone.

Hebrews: one road

We step out with confidence because we've discovered someone who makes that possible. However long the road seems, wherever it goes, we don't travel alone. Jesus is with us, breathing through everything we do, bringing us close to God. Our belief isn't a set of rules; our trust is in Jesus, who is the same yesterday, today and forever.

James:
you say it's real, show me

The James in the title of this letter may well be the one who is the brother of Jesus and who became a leader of the church in Jerusalem. It seems to be written mainly for Christians from a Jewish background. And, if you like practical advice, this is where you'll find it.

There's not a lot to be said, for or against a mouth… until you put a tongue in it. Then all kinds of mischief or marvels can break out. It's all down to how people use it. That's why you don't want anyone and everyone teaching about the Christian faith.

Words are dynamite and it's just so easy to make mistakes. An out-of-control tongue is like a burning match in a tinder-dry forest. Once the bad stuff starts, you never know where it's going to end. People can be nice as pie one minute and cursing you the next. It doesn't add up… and it shouldn't happen.

Stay sure

That's a flavour of the letter from James, who does gritty, practical stuff – like how you keep going on the grey days when you're up against it. But there's more to him than that. James knows how important faith is, but he wants to be sure it actually exists. If you say you love God, then spend lots of time being unpleasant to other people, you need to think again about who you claim to be.

He's writing to challenge and encourage Christians who are facing hard times. God will give you what you need, he writes, so long as you keep going. Don't let doubt creep in, or you become like a wave that's tossed every which way in a storm. Good things *will* come from God. The only thing he doesn't offer is temptation. That's something which slides in under the door when your mind's elsewhere and then slowly suffocates the life out of you. Don't blame God for that.

We're here for a short while. Your good looks won't last, neither will your money. What matters most then? What God plants in your heart. That's what gives birth to the good fruit in your life – things like being a good listener, cautious with opinions and slow to anger.

Put love into practice. If you listen to God's word but don't follow it, it's like looking at yourself in a mirror and immediately forgetting what you've seen. But if you look at what God says and act on it, happiness can meet you on any corner.

Evidence

Don't treat others differently because of their looks or their bank balance, and don't expect mercy if you aren't merciful. Love others as you love yourself. That's what scripture teaches. God isn't looking for people who just avoid mistakes, but for people who give help where it's needed.

James knows that saying you have faith doesn't prove anything; you need the evidence. If you've got food and clothes when those around you haven't, it's no good going: 'God bless you and keep you warm.' Do something about it.

Abraham didn't just pray. He got out there, walked God's road. Wisdom isn't simply what you know; it's what you do with that knowledge. Some people use cleverness to create jealousy, to strengthen their own position or simply to cause trouble. God's wisdom is about purity, about selflessness. It's a peaceful and gentle companion, an honest and unprejudiced guide. You know it by the sunshine it creates.

What drives us

Fights and quarrels break out where you let evil have the upper hand. Then people become driven by what they want and will do all sorts of things to get it. If you want God's help, get close to him and he will come close to you. He will lift you up if you can only recognise how far you have fallen.

Don't criticise others – God is the only judge. Don't boast of your own schemes, rattling on about making the next million while not paying people the wages they're due. The clock of your life is ticking, so be grateful for each day: it is God's gift. If time is on your side, don't waste it on growing rich and getting big; dedicate it to fairness and helpfulness.

And be patient. Things don't happen all at once. Look at the seasons that farmers have to get through before the harvest comes. We all suffer pain and, like Job, trouble sometimes seems to go on forever. But God came through for him and he'll do the same for you.

Be straightforward. Let your 'yes' be 'yes' and your 'no' be 'no'. If you're in trouble, pray – it's powerful. If you're happy, celebrate the fact. If you're ill, ask others to pray for you. Be honest when you're at fault – it's the road to healing. Look out for those you love and bring each other back when you drift into bad ways. That takes you to the best place of all – the house of forgiveness.

A taste of James

What you do matters. Talking about faith doesn't prove anything. If you speak badly about everyone but claim to be good, that doesn't add up. Be patient, listen well, pay people properly. Put love into practice by helping out where you can. Look at what God says and do it – that's where blessings begin.

1 Peter:
stick with it

Simon Peter was the disciple who Jesus called his 'rock' and who became a key leader in the early church. This is a newsletter to those under pressure for their faith. That could mean losing your job, getting kicked out of the family home, being imprisoned or even killed. So it's not surprising to find the letter majors on the practical rather than the philosophical.

Even in bad times, there are reasons to be thankful, and one of them is the living hope that Jesus brings, a life where nothing spoils, where nothing fades away. These are hard times at the moment but it will prove you're genuine. You love Jesus, even though you've never seen him, because you sense in your heart and soul what he has done for you.

More than you used to be

Keep on the right track with God. Love one another with all your heart, all your strength. You are twice the person you once were. Here, we're like flowers that shrivel and fade across the days but, with the breath of God in us, we will be always new, every morning.

Clear out the bad stuff: lies, jealousy, insults, fake holiness. Stay as keen on learning about God as a baby is about its milk. Be rock solid for Jesus. Don't let the wrong desires take over. Live as free people, but don't think that you can do whatever you like. Serve God, love others, respect everyone.

Do right by your bosses, whether they treat you well or not. Don't forget, when Christ was treated badly, he didn't spend all his time shouting at people or threatening them. Neither should you. He was wounded so that you might be healed and brought home by the keeper of your soul.

Stay with it

Husbands and wives should care *about* each other and *for* each other. It's about being beautiful people deep down, showing understanding and respect for the one you married. God loves each of you equally.

Don't let fear strangle the joy out of life. Care for one another as family; pay back evil with good and do not be afraid of anyone. Christ is your heartbeat, so let him lead your life. Tell others what keeps you hopeful. Speak gently and respect where people are in their lives.

You are different now. Even if you're suffering, you've put the bad stuff in your life behind you. Instead, you're stepping out with a different kind of love: opening your homes, using your talents, making the most of what God has created you to be. That can be tough to do at times, but be glad that you are being faithful to the creator of all.

If you're a church leader, don't start bossing other people about. Be an example and serve them well. Don't think about what you can get but what you can give. If you're younger, listen to those with experience and be willing to learn from them. And, if you've got worries, leave them with God.

Stay sharp and give evil the big 'no'. Be firm in your faith. When you're feeling pain, understand that you are not alone.

Silas has been a big help in writing this and here's the heart of the matter: the love that God showers upon us is what makes the difference. Watch out, stay close to Jesus, stick with it and may peace be with you.

1 Peter in a nutshell

What Jesus did means we can start all over again with him as our heartbeat. We should be the ones who help keep the world turning. Life can be tough here, so hold tight to your faith and respect others because we're travelling with God now and forever. Everything in this world shrivels and dies across time… but what Jesus gives us is always there, always fresh, always new.

2 Peter:
get a grip

A little letter to a wide circle of Christians, reminding them to trust Jesus. It may be brief, but it has three great qualities: it's down-to-earth, helpful and hopeful.

Do we need big houses? Or enormous bank balances? No, says Peter's second letter, what matters is the power God gives us to live life to the full. That requires three basic ingredients: faith, courage and common sense. Add to them a grip on what you're doing and a determination to keep going. Fold in the sunshine you can see in someone who's close to God, a real affection for each other and a love for all of God's creation. Then, you've got the recipe for life as it's meant to be.

Without these things, you're someone who squints and stumbles through this world, unable to see all the good that God has done. With them, you're turning those first steps with God into a faith that will stand the test of time.

The real thing

We don't make up what we say; we were actually there. In the past, prophets gave us a glimpse of light in dark times. Now, Jesus shines like the morning star into the depths of our hearts.

Don't listen to dangerous nonsense like the idea that Christ didn't save you. Watch out as well for those who have a tight grip on cash and a loose grip on morals. Some people will say anything to make money out of you.

God isn't going to put up with behaviour like this. He didn't in the past and he isn't going to start now. The pleasure seekers think they're free but, in reality, they're trapped. Be different. Think about what is pure and right.

Time and God

Whatever predictions you've heard about the future, stay close to God, who keeps his promises both now and always. Then everything that is kind and true and fair will find its home.

I know some things are difficult to understand, says Peter. Paul's letters contain things that can be hard, and people take the opportunity to claim they mean all sorts of strange things about the end of time. What's important is to keep with God's promises and live a good life. Go on growing closer to him, understanding him better, loving him more.

Life according to 2 Peter

Be brave, be sensible, have faith, keep going. Love God and all his creation, including each other. Don't fret about what might happen at the end of time. Focus on how Jesus brings us into relationship with God and lights up each day of our life, keeping his promises both now and always.

1 John:
the real Jesus

Early references suggest this letter is from John, one of the twelve disciples. He sees people who started out so well but have been distracted by strange ideas. John sets out to get his readers back on track.

It's what we've seen, heard and touched, and it was there from the beginning of time. This is what we keep talking about and why we want you to join us. Life with God the Father and Jesus his Son is extraordinary. God is light and in him there is no darkness at all. If we belong to God, our ways are lit by him. At the same time, we need to be honest about our failure. God forgives us and makes us clean again, but first we have to own up to the mess we make.

That's how John begins. He's writing to churches where some people have become a sort of super-spiritual club for 'clever' people who think they deserve to be treated as first-class Christians. John explains that prayer always needs to be partnered by care and there's only one class of travel with Jesus – family class.

Being real

This letter is a reality check. Say you're following God but do exactly what you like? You're a liar. Reckon you can love God while hating people? That's like standing in a pitch-black room and pretending it's full of light.

You've come so far. Don't get sucked in by the 'want, want, want' culture around you. It isn't going to last. Instead, write on your heart that Jesus brings life both now and forever. Remember that and stay close to him. God loves us so much he calls us his children.

Voices and actions

We put our hope in Christ and so keep ourselves in the best shape we can. Be loving even if everyone else seems to be fighting and only looking out for themselves. But don't be surprised if you're not popular with some people because of this. Love is about letting go of your own life for others, like Christ did. It's the road we follow. You can't be a Christian and close your heart to other people's needs. You can't just talk about love; you have to live it.

It's not just about feelings, either. If you listen to your conscience, you may well feel you're never good enough for God. But faith doesn't depend on our emotions, only on what God does. That's greater than any voice in your head making you feel you're no good.

Love at the max

Some people will say that Jesus was never really a human being but just looked like one. The truth is the very opposite of that. He came as flesh and blood. So let us love one another because love comes from God. Then you're living wholeheartedly as God's family. Remember, it's not that we have loved God, but that he loved us so much that he sent his Son as the way in which our sins are forgiven.

God is love, and when we love each other and have his Spirit at work in us, we show his love to this world. There is nothing to be afraid of here. True love has the power to drive out fear. We know God hears our prayers and that he cares for us.

We love because God loved us first, so we need to show that love to each other. We can do this if we stick with Jesus and keep on believing.

Some of those you meet will have taken a wrong road. If there is the tiniest chance of a way back for them, pray with all your heart that they may find it. God's family isn't perfect, but Jesus pulls us back and keeps us from getting trapped on the dark side. Our place is with him and with each other. There are lots of other voices out there. Don't drift with the tide. Keep yourselves safe.

---

1 John: what love is and isn't

- Love isn't about being especially spiritual; it's about being God's children.

- Love never says, 'You're not good enough'; instead it says, 'You can be forgiven.'

- Love means not drifting with the tide but staying close to Jesus.

- Love isn't about us taking charge but about God leading our lives.

Home
Exile
Love
Faith
Home

Home
Exile
Love
Faith
Home

Home
Exile
Love
Faith
Home

Home
Exile
Love
Faith
Home

2 John:
keep love going

A personal note to a lady he holds dear and her children – this may mean a local church. John refers to himself as 'the elder' in this letter. If it's John, the disciple, he'd be in his 80s by the time this was written.

Blessings upon you all: peace, mercy and love without limit. So happy to hear about how you keep following God's way. Go on doing it, loving one another, getting on with what we were called to do and who we were called to be.

Did Jesus actually come as a real, flesh and blood, human being? Absolutely! There was no trick of the light making him seem other than what he was. Don't let anyone tell you different. If they go beyond what Christ taught, they go beyond God. Don't listen to them – it's a fraud.

A letter is good, but I'm hoping to visit you soon as there's so much to say. Everyone sends their love.

2 John: the shorter-than-short version

- Is Jesus real? Absolutely.
- Do peace, love and mercy have limits? Absolutely not.
- So be who you were called to be.

3 John:
the difference you make

At not much more than 200 words in the original Greek, this is the shortest book in the Bible but one with a classic contrast between two kinds of people.

Dear Gaius

I hope and pray you're in good health and that everything's going well. It was great to hear how faithful you are in following Christ. You're a caring friend and I was thrilled to hear from others that you're the same with total strangers as with me. How good is that! Keep on welcoming travellers. That's one way we share together in our work for the truth.

I wrote to the church, but Diotrephes, who loves being in charge, will not welcome us. Be aware of what he is up to. He doesn't listen, makes up all kinds of stories, hasn't got a welcome for other Christians and tries to stop those who have. What is his problem? Don't imitate him, whatever you do.

Follow the right examples. Like Demetrius: nobody's got a bad word to say about him. That's a reputation we think he deserves. No more from my pen. The rest can wait until we meet. Soon, I hope! From all of us here, greetings and peace.

3 John: a life lesson

Following Christ means being the one with the welcome. We don't need people who love being in charge; we need people who love being there for others.

Jude:
taking advantage

Jude is the name of one of Jesus' four brothers. His older brother James became the leader of the church in Jerusalem. We know very little about this letter, but it deals with a very common problem.

This is a letter that its author would prefer not to be writing. I wanted to tell you all about what a joy salvation is, admits Jude, but people seem to have sneaked into your group who think they can do what they like and use Christ's grace and forgiveness as a way to allow bad behaviour.

God doesn't stand by while everyone does what they like. Think about people and places in our history like Sodom and Gomorrah – they disappeared altogether. Now you've got members who dream up justifications for anything. They're blots on the landscape, promising what they never deliver and are only interested in themselves. That's when they're not whingeing, moaning and blaming others!

These are the ones who don't like doing what they're told but do make a big noise about what they claim they've achieved. Then they use flattery to get round you. The breath of God isn't in them, but the ability to cause trouble is.

Pray and keep yourself deep in the power of God's Spirit and love. Go easy on people who have doubts, help those who are tempted but don't drift yourself. Turn your eyes upon the one who can keep you from falling and bring you shining into his wonderful presence. That's our God, who works this miracle through Jesus, our amazing Lord of yesterday, today and forever.

Jude in short

Forgiveness isn't a free pass to go on doing what you like. Don't let anyone excuse bad behaviour by blaming others. Instead, turn your eyes upon Jesus and let him bring you into the light, not just for a moment but for eternity.

Home
Exile
Love
Faith
Home

Home
Exile
Love
Faith
Home

Home
Exile
Love
Faith
Home

Home
Exile
Love
Faith
Home

Revelation:
where all our journeys end

The story behind Revelation is this: a man called John gets banished to the island of Patmos as punishment for preaching and starts to see visions. Now the trouble with dreams is when people read too much into them, and John gives a sharp warning about this. So remember the simple core of what John writes here – that God, whose breath was there at the beginning, will still be there at the very last moment of time.

There are two main elements to John's dreams in Revelation. The opening part is straightforward. It's the stuff of prophets: seven messages from God for the surrounding churches. Then, all that's weird and wonderful kicks in. But first, there's the short messages about how the people are doing here and now.

Ephesus is a good place for hard work, patience and doing the right thing but the passion has gone. You couldn't call the people idle, but they don't love God as they once did. 'Go back to the beginning,' is the call to them: 'Remember who you once were.'

Trouble and poverty have hit those in Smyrna but it will not be the end. 'Don't be afraid,' they're told, 'hold on and you'll come through.'

Life has had its tragedies for the Christians in Pergamum, too, but they haven't given up. Some people have drifted into bad ways and need to stop or face the consequences. Those who are faithful will find hidden depths of strength.

People are patient, caring and loving in Thyatira, but they tolerate at least one person who is the absolute opposite. If they take the path where darkness beckons, it will swallow them; if they stick by all that's good, they will grow strong and be bright stars in this world.

Sardis has a good reputation and doesn't deserve it. Christ's followers do plenty, but the flame that fires their lives burns low. Some people here are in the right place with God. It's time for the rest to wake-up and join them.

In Philadelphia, the church isn't strong or successful, but most of them have done what they were called to do. So the door is open and, as weak as people feel, they'll walk through it into a bright eternity.

Laodicea is rich and successful but its members don't grasp what faith means. They're lukewarm: God is like an optional extra. These people *can* be part of the picture but, first, they have to want to be. God stands at the door and knocks: if they hear his voice and open the door, he will come in and be with them. But it's no good someone knocking if you don't open the door.

Weird but wonderful

That's the bit everyone can follow. The next part is John's vision of people continuing to worship in the midst of chaos and confusion. The first surprise is that this is worship with the sparkle factor fully in place: thrones, jewels, rainbows, torches. Perhaps that's because there's no better time to be hopeful and grateful than when everything is against you.

The focus of the dream swings wildly between extraordinary celebrations of praise and monstrous chaos. There's a beast with seven heads plus ten horns, and locusts the size of horses with teeth like lions and stings like scorpions. In the midst of all this, John sees Christ as the lamb. It's a symbol of innocence and sacrifice in the midst of what seems like the end of the world.

In reality, it isn't the end because John has already called Jesus the beginning and the end. Instead, those who have created chaos will be destroyed by it. The Roman Empire will fall and the authorities that have banned John will sink like a millstone into the sea.

The old and the new

Finally, there's a day when everyone is called to account. For some, John sees a second death. For others, he sees redemption: a new heaven, a new earth, a new city. God is with his people at last, wiping away every tear from their eyes. No more crying, no more grief, no more death.

'I am making all things new,' God explains. 'It's done. I am the beginning and the end. The spring from which the water of life flows is for you. Drink freely for I will be your God and you will be my child.'

The offer isn't exclusive and it's free. This is a new world without dark corners, a life beyond shadows. John finishes with a reminder that the invitation to come to God is for everyone and a warning that his book is not there to be turned into something that it isn't. So the Bible draws to a close. In the beginning, God creates… in the end, he makes all things new again.

Messages from Revelation

Remember who you once were and how you were forgiven. Hold on and you'll come through like stars that light the dark night sky. When God calls, open the door as he makes all things new again. Out of chaos comes a world without grief. Step out of the shadows. Choose life.

Further reading

Bible translations

Almost everyone has a favourite and all translations have their strengths and weaknesses. You can explore the mind-boggling variety at **biblegateway.com**, with over 50 choices at your fingertips and that's not all of them! Often I'll start with New Revised Standard Version (NRSV) and the New International Version (NIV), turning to the Contemporary English Version (CEV) and the Good News Bible (GNT) for clarity in reading aloud. The Message (MSG) is also fascinating because it's Eugene Peterson's individual translation for the people he knew and loved across 30 years as their pastor.

Bible notes

In theory, you don't need study notes in order to read the Bible but, for most people, they're a real help. I actually started with BRF's Bible reading notes so long ago I don't want to admit to the actual date. Then I needed a change and went to *The Upper Room*, a very different kind of approach also published by BRF. Later I enjoyed *Disclosure*: hilarious, sometimes controversial and sadly no longer available. They all worked for me in different ways.

You can take a look at a range of choices from BRF at **brfonline.org.uk/our-notes**. Scripture Union is another option; you can see their daily reading resources at **content.scriptureunion.org.uk**. Notes work in creating a pattern for learning. It may also help to try a different series from time to time.

Study Bibles

These are big and often expensive, but if you like explanations and thoughts alongside your Bible reading, one of them could make an excellent present. The bestseller is the *NIV Life Applications Study Bible* (Hodder and Stoughton, 2017), but many of the translations have a version with notes alongside the text. If you can manage it, this is one decision that is probably best taken in a shop where you can see exactly what you're getting.

Studies on individual books

These are most often turned to by people leading Bible study groups or worship. Like Bibles themselves, they come in all shapes and sizes. 'The Really Useful Guides' from BRF are short, fresh and accessible. More detail is provided by the 'For Everyone' series published by SPCK. The New Testament books are covered there by Tom Wright and the Old Testament by John Goldingay. Whatever series is chosen, people sometimes find that they have bought books that are too detailed for their needs. So, if you can, take a look before parting with cash.

Reference books

Arguably, the best starting point if you want a book to fill in the background for you is *The Bible Book: A user's guide* by Nick Page (HarperCollins, 2002). This offers you plenty of information and sums up disagreements about a text in a clear, accessible form. It also points out the tricky bits and what people have made of them. Helpful, witty and blissfully brief!

A different kind of reference is provided by *Journey Through the Bible* (Lion Hudson, 2021), which provides a highly visual background to over 200 of the main stories from the Bible. Packed with photographs, diagrams, maps and charts.

Equally colourful but with substantially more detail is *The Lion Handbook to the Bible* (Lion Hudson, 2017, fifth edition). This focuses on the books rather than the stories. The advertising copy describes it as 'a mine of information' and on this occasion that seems very fair.

Finally, if you can unearth a copy of *The Complete Bible Handbook* by John Bowker (Dorling Kindersley, 2004), you'll be rewarded by a volume that deals well with many of the difficult subjects like slavery, sacrifice and suffering as well as good coverage of the individual books.

Issues – violence

The worlds of the Old Testament and the New Testament sometimes seem to be a universe apart. *God of Violence Yesterday, God of Love Today?* by Helen Paynter (BRF, 2019) deals freshly and honestly with what to make of the violence in the Old Testament. Worth a read especially because it doesn't skirt around the issue.

Issues – suffering

This is always one of the hard questions that religions have to face. The fact that it can appear so random and unfair can ruin people's faith. Even Job doesn't solve everyone's dilemmas about it. One book worth looking at is *Disappointment with God* by Philip Yancey (Zondervan, 1988). The second part, 'Seeing in the Dark', is particularly gripping. And, if you read only one chapter, make it the one headed 'Is God unfair?'.

Issues – the role of women

Many traditional assumptions about the role of women in the Bible can be misleading or simply inaccurate. *Daughters of Eve* by Martyn and Esther Whittock (Lion Books, 2021) provides a refreshing look at the history. Taking a different angle, *Unveiled* by Clare and Micah Hayns (BRF, 2021) introduces 40 women of the Old Testament across 40 days of reflections with honesty, wit and stunning artwork. Two new ways of thinking that complement each other.

Going deeper

Books which deal with how to understand the Bible also deserve their place on people's shelves. *How to Read the Bible... so that it makes a difference* by Michael Parsons (BRF, 2020) is a good place to start the process of trying to see things more clearly and as they were intended to be seen. If you fancy something slightly more academic, you might try *How to Read the Bible for All Its Worth* by Gordon Fee and Douglas Stuart (Zondervan, 1982). Eye-opening if you worry a lot about getting hold of the wrong end of the stick and excellent on parables. It also tells you whether it's absolutely necessary to greet each other with a holy kiss as Paul suggests!

Acknowledgements

It was Rob Lacey, who wrote *The Word on the Street* (Zondervan, 2005), who got me started on all this. He had a picture of other voices, dozens perhaps, all saying what they heard when they read the Bible. In my case, he was particularly keen to know what I could make of Leviticus. Rob and I had such fun amid the sad and painful times of his last years that I hope he's smiling down on this.

A massive word of thanks to Shirley Wakley and all who read or heard sections and commented: lots of details were clarified in that way. When I was still unsure, I phoned Revd Donald Ker to chew over the matter. Such a reassurance to speak with a man who props his Greek New Testament against his box of cornflakes. Don's common sense and understanding of nuance helped when books didn't.

This book was only ever meant to be a start and an encouragement. In different ways, everyone has a role in shedding light on the world. If you believe that, even slightly, then this poem is for you and about you.

We are the night-shifters:
the ones at work when others are asleep,
the team that tries to take the strain
wherever pain has gone too deep.

We are the load-bearers:
the ones who see that no one walks alone.
We're not the quick-solutionists;
who answer with a megaphone.

We are the dawn-breakers:
the ones who trust the nightmare has an end.
We've come and we intend to stay;
we're here to heal, to hold, to mend.

We are the night-shifters:
the ones who've learnt to laugh and cry and pray.
We try to make this where love lives,
to turn each shred of darkness into day.

Life on film

They want some footage of my life
For the publicity campaign.
I sit in the garden and write this.
What a strange thing to be doing:
Re-enacting my private life
For public consumption.

It's not false: this is what I do
But it's not entirely true either:
I know a camera's following me
And I pretend to be unaware of it.
The difference between
This afternoon and reality
Is that life happens
Without any chance to edit it.

Life doesn't let you choose,
The angle at which the light catches your face,
Nor does it dwell lovingly on your better side.
It ambushes you, raw and unprepared,
For nearly every scene that unfolds
In ways you never planned for or expected.

That's why it's good to give
Each other second chances.
If we cannot edit life,
We should at least live it
With kindness and forgiveness.
There will be no repeat performance.